PRAISE FOR *COMPETITIVE PE(*

"The importance of a forward-thinking, comprehensive people strategy to underpin our business strategies has never been more important. Kevin lends his experience and insights from many years as a business and HR leader to challenge as well as provide great practical advice on all aspects of people strategy, and the innovations needed in HR practices to help people and organizations to thrive in a fast-changing future."
Peter Cheese, Chief Executive, CIPD

"This book is an A to Z for HR professionals. It offers an all-encompassing approach which shows how joined-up thinking in relation to people can lead to business success. Confronting and energizing in equal measure."
Alison Hodgson, VP People, Virgin Media Ireland

"In this book, Kevin brings a unique perspective to the strategic opportunities organizations can achieve through their people. Providing insight and direction not just for people practitioners, but for anyone leading an organization who has questions about how to better drive performance and productivity."
Neil Morrison, Director of HR, Severn Trent

"A must-read book for all leaders, articulating the steps to creating a competitive people strategy for commercial and ultimately broader social good. AI is changing the face of work, creating more flexibility and a greater ease of removing the mundane, but there is a heightened need for creativity, innovation and intuition, which can only come from an engaged, energized and committed workforce."
Helen Pitcher OBE, Chairman of Advanced Boardroom Excellence, President INSEAD Directors Network, NED and Remuneration Committee Chair, C&C Group PLC, and Chairman, Criminal Cases Review Commission

"Kevin clearly outlines the importance of driving a coherent strategy in order to compete in an increasingly difficult labour market – where a business cannot be afraid to self-disrupt and diversify their offerings if they are to thrive, attract and retain talent. People and effective use of technology are at the heart of this and *Competitive People Strategy* underscores the all-too-common pitfalls to avoid and the real commercial and social upside of getting this right."
Bill Richards, UK Managing Director, Indeed

"An insightful and engaging look at the role people play in the success of businesses, especially if they are motivated, organized and utilized in the right ways. Kevin talks from a position of authority having spent a lifetime in this arena, as a CEO, HRD and also as a thought leader and change agent. A great read!"
Chris Moore, Chairman, Recruitment and Employment Confederation

"At a time when the workforce is becoming more dispersed, remote and diverse, building and leading communities of workers will become one of the key disciplines of 21st-century business. This book provides inspiring insights in how to implement a total talent management strategy to improve performance and retain your talent".
Denis Pennel, Managing Director, World Employment Confederation

"Kevin distils, codifies and then crafts the necessary focus on the future of work's undeniable constant: people. It's all about the people. No longer will people say 'I'm not sure what to do about my people strategy' because it's all in this book. Enough guidance, enough back story and enough stimulation to just go and do it. So, if in doubt about the status of your people strategy, check in with this book and check out with Kevin's series of tools, recommendations and tactics."
Perry Timms, author of *Transformational HR*

"The right people strategy is critical to business success. This book provides an invaluable insight into why this is the case and the thinking and approaches that are available to businesses to get the most out of their people. It is a must-read for HR Directors and CEOs alike."
Martin Hesketh, CEO, Brookson

"In this book, strategy meets people in a mix of practical steps and guided learning which will supercharge your approach to leadership and talent. Kevin brings a wealth of experience to the alignment of your employee experience to enable you to achieve your business outcomes. A must-read for all people-centric leaders."
Aaron Alburey, Founder and CEO, Lace Partners

"This book is a great and pragmatic read which responds to the issues organizations are confronted with. Kevin makes astute observations together with practical tools to assist with the ever-growing number of workplace challenges. This is not a boring corporate HR read – Kevin has solicited views and opinions and offers a practical set of solutions for HR professionals to raise their game and continue to integrate HR plans with the business strategy."
Jacky Simmonds, Group Chief People Officer, Veon PLC

"This book provides many practical tips to help HR practitioners link their work to their business strategy and build a differentiated approach that creates competitive advantage through their people. I have personally benefited from using the Three Key Questions."
Quintin Heath, HRD, AB Sugar

"A powerful toolkit and an inspiring read for anyone looking to scale their organization via their people."
Terence Mauri, *Inc.* Magazine Writer and bestselling author of
The Leader's Mindset

"This is an excellent book for any leader who wants to achieve superior business results while also building a great place to work. It's full of sound business advice and practical ideas of how to get the best from your people."
Steve Ingham, Group CEO, Page Group Plc

"This is a great book for those looking to give their people strategy an edge, whether they are a CEO or HRD. It's an easy read, very accessible and clearly articulates its key point that the most valuable people strategy is not one based on best practice, but rather one that puts a

focus on a doing things differently. Kevin Green's refreshing message is essentially 'find a small number of things that can authentically set your organization apart from the rest, and do them brilliantly'."
Ralph Tribe, Chief People Officer, Ascential PLC

"It is a cliché, but nevertheless true, that there is a war for talent. Kevin Green has been in the trenches of that war for longer than most. He is also a clear and entertaining communicator, so his opinions are well worth reading."
Calum Chase, author of *Surviving AI*

"Kevin is an HR professional with a difference – in his book he debunks the myth that all leaders should be extrovert salesmen and explains how to pull together the component parts of successful people strategy – all leaders of people should take note."
Mark Palmer, CEO, Gobeyond Partners UK

"People, culture and organizational design are critical to understanding when making investment decisions. Getting it right or wrong can, and so often does, define an investment outcome. This book shows leaders how great people engagement can achieve superior business returns."
Dawn Marriott Sims, Partner, Hg

"Winning in business is all about creating a competitive edge, and in Kevin's book he succinctly defines how to do this. He also takes us through how leaders should deal with the changes occurring in the modern workforce. This book explains how leaders can attract, motivate, engage and retain their talent. It's a must-read."
Peter Searle, Executive Chairman, Airswift PLC

"In *Competitive People Strategy* Kevin Green brings HR kicking and screaming into the 21st century – and shows every HR and business leader how to compete and win in the midst of the fourth Industrial Revolution."
Colin Donnery, General Manager, FRS Recruitment

"Kevin has cracked the code, successfully smashing the disciplines of business strategy and people management together, which is where they have always truly belonged. He provides a cogent formula across the entire people and organizational performance lifecycle, creating a timely call to arms and a practical pathway for leaders and change agents around the globe to create a far greater impact."

Steve Bernard, Founder and Managing Director, Connectwell

Competitive People Strategy

*How to attract, develop and retain
the staff you need for business success*

Kevin Green

KoganPage

First published in Great Britain and the United States in 2019 by Kogan Page Limited

2nd Floor, 45 Gee Street
London
EC1V 3RS
United Kingdom

122 W 27th St, 10th Floor
New York, NY 10001
USA

4737/23 Ansari Road
Daryaganj
New Delhi 110002
India

www.koganpage.com

ISBNs

Hardback   9780749498528
Paperback   9780749484545
Ebook   9780749484552

British Library Cataloguing-in-Publication Data

A CIP record for this book is available from the British Library.

Library of Congress Cataloging-in-Publication Data

A CIP record for this book is available from the Library of Congress.

Typeset by Integra
Print production managed by Jellyfish
Printed and bound in Great Britain by Ashford Colour Press Ltd.

To the two loves of my life, my wife Sharon and my son Tom,
thanks for all the love, support and guidance.

And to all the leaders and HR professionals trying
to grow a business via your people – keep stretching
to make a difference. It will be worth it.

CONTENTS

FIGURES

PREFACE

The world of work is changing fast, driven by advances in technology, labour market polarization, social attitudes and political upheavals. It's also true that at the same time businesses secure more of their competitive advantage from people than at any other time in history. However, very few organizations know how to craft a people strategy that makes a significant difference to their business performance. Even fewer are executing a people strategy that will improve their competitiveness by leading, managing and developing their people more effectively than their competitors.

The people advantage has come about as businesses recognize that it's ideas, creativity, brands, relationships and agility that will enable them to compete and win in today's hyper competitive markets. Whereas in previous eras commercial success was about access to capital, primarily to invest in plant and machinery, it's now all about the skill, talent and capability of your people, individually and collectively. People are the wealth creators now. Businesses that are able to leverage their culture and talent will be able to create a sustainable competitive advantage.

The vast majority of business leaders and human resources practitioners do not know, and have never been shown, how to create a Competitive People Strategy. It isn't widely taught and there are few great case studies. The science shows that those organizations that think, plan and execute a strategy focused on maximizing their human potential will have a distinct advantage in the decade ahead.

This book is a call to arms to business leaders who want their organizations to grow, make greater profit and outperform their competitors. It will show you how to achieve those objectives by becoming a great place to work. This book will demonstrate how devising and executing a Competitive People Strategy will separate you from the herd, and provide a sustainable and defendable advantage while focusing your business on people interventions that make a difference.

Our changing workforce and why now is the time to create a Competitive People Strategy

Two giant workplace shifts are taking place at the same time. First, individuals with the talent and skills demanded by employers have more choice than ever. They can choose not just whom they work for, but how they work. Many of these talented individuals may choose to be employed, run their own business or become a freelancer, contractor or consultant. Many now choose to work part-time. The talented have more choice to balance their life, undertake meaningful work while also controlling their own destiny. They are utilizing the power of the market to provide them with opportunities for meaningful work in the most convenient format. To attract, hire and retain this talent, businesses need to provide a great experience and, as a consequence, think much more deeply about purpose, culture and leadership behaviour than at any time since organizations were first created.

A recent study by the Staffing Industry Analysts shows that in many large multinational businesses only 66 per cent of the workforce are permanent employees, the rest being temps, contractors, freelancers and consultants (SIA, 2018). That's 34 per cent of your workforce who provide value to your customers but who perceive themselves to be a gun for hire. This will increase as businesses start to engage talent in many more forms. How do you build a people strategy when much of your talent and skill is not actually employed by the organization?

Today's companies are seeking to be more agile and responsive to customers' wants and needs. The desire for greater skill and talent while at the same time keeping costs under control means organizations are deploying new workforce strategies. This leads to businesses bringing in capability just in time to meet and fulfil projects or respond to changes in customer demand. This creates the need for a people strategy for the whole workforce, not just your direct employees. No business can afford to treat their flexible resource as a commodity. You want to build a culture which engages, develops and keeps flexible talent wanting to come back to work in your business.

Second, organizations in mature labour markets are suffering with shortages of skill and talent. A 2018 survey by PWC (the professional services organization) of global chief executive officers (CEOs) shows that 80 per cent are concerned with a shortage of skills and talent. This was, by some distance, their number one issue. In a separate survey the Confederation of British Industry (CBI) (2018) recently found that 56 per cent of employers are struggling to fill all the jobs they have available. So, while businesses in all sectors and of different sizes are finding it tough to find the right people, they are using contractors, freelancers and consultants to plug the gaps and resource important work.

This trend is being amplified by the way professional and managerial work is being organized within businesses. Organizational structures are becoming more fluid and agile, so project working and matrix management structures are now the norm. These new ways of working, aligned to the shortages, are encouraging firms to become more creative with their workforce design and placing more emphasis on providing a great work experience.

This book will help business and people leaders think strategically about people and define how to craft a differentiated people strategy that enables your business to be more successful. The first three chapters are about business strategy itself and how to craft a Competitive People Strategy. The following six chapters (on leadership, culture, talent and hiring, employee engagement and experience, change and transformation, and people management) are the areas of focus in a Competitive People Strategy. Finally, there is a chapter on the people or HR function itself and how it should up its game or become a support function forever.

The book aims to help people practitioners immerse themselves in how businesses compete and how to then develop innovative ways of hiring, developing, engaging and rewarding your people that are fully aligned to the achievement of the business goals and objectives.

It also shows how great HR interventions that are aligned to the business' strategy will eliminate once and for all the 'one size fits all' approach of HR good practice. Leaders and people practitioners need to stop hiding behind their organizations policies, practices and procedures that often add cost and complexity without any discernible business benefit.

The future belongs to organizations that can build a culture, where individuals are recognized for their unique talent, where great team work is an everyday experience and where people understand why what they do every day, matters. The power of getting every person in an organization to give their best is at the heart of this book.

How this book works

At the start of each chapter I explain the concept and idea. At the end of each chapter I highlight questions for you and your colleagues to consider in relation to your organization. Think of it as your leadership checklist.

In most chapters I have provided case studies or examples of organizations that are starting to put people first and are getting the commercial returns. Also included, wherever possible, are practical tools so you can start putting them into practice immediately. I hope you enjoy the book.

References

CBI/Pertemps (2018) Employment Trends Survey 2018
  www.pertemps.co.uk/employers/resource-centre/employment-trends-survey/
  employment-trends-survey-2018/
PWC (2018) 21st CEO survey, the talent challenge: Rebalancing skills for the
  digital age
  www.pwc.com/gx/en/ceo-survey/2018/deep-dives/pwc-ceo-survey-talent.pdf
SIA (2018) Workforce solutions buyer survey www2.staffingindustry.com/row/
  Research/Research-Reports/APAC/Buyer-Survey-APAC-2018-Full

ACKNOWLEDGEMENTS

I would like to thank lots of people. This book is the result of thirty-eight years of business experience.

To the team at Qtab: my partner in crime Sue Higgins and my dream team of consultants Helen Hatton, Jane Heath, Kevin Deed, Trevor Croucher (keep kicking arse), Amita Sandhu, Darrell Oakley and Ralph Tribe (a leading thinker on competing with your people). Plus Robin Bowden for helping keep the wheels on the road.

Team Royal Mail: to Adam Cozier and Tony McCarthy for giving me the chance to do something big. To the operators, the first among equals being Big Tom Melvin plus Paul Tolhurst, Tony Fox, James Farren, Roger Baynes, Paul Budd and Steve Cameron. To the HR top team: Dermot Toberty, Julie Welch, Vikki Hawes, Amanda Stone, Karen Brinkman, Helen Atkinson, Amanda Strickland, Jane Mee, Sarah Wagnall, Peter Wilkinson, Alison Hodgson, Jayne Lewis and Pamela Stephenson plus the late and great Mark Robertson for keeping us all on track – you're still solely missed. We did something remarkable.

To the Rec Crew. To my four chairs: thanks for being there and supporting me thorough thick and thin. First the pocket dynamo Angela Masters, Neil Smith (let's not talk about the curry), Simon Noakes and Chris Moore. The top team: David Vallance, Richard Charnock, Peter Copus, Steve Othen, Tom Hadley, Martin Noble, Fiona Coombe, Kate Shoesmith, the PR guru Liz Banks, and Anita Holbrow (the one that should have followed). Plus my old muckers Carol Scott, Chris Howard, Angie Nichoals and Karen Williams (my West Wing buddy, we will never forget those naan breads!). Those that sorted me out every day: Sadie Jones (now and then!), Selina Barry Jones and Gemma Donaldson. The pleasure was all mine!

The international WEC family: Denis Pennel, Brettina Schaller, Annemarie Muntz, Charles Cameron, Richard Wahlquist, Michal Feytang, Jakob Tietge, Even Hagelien, Tuliara Merru, Geraldine King, Frank Farrelly and Barbara McGrath and Jon Healy.

To my HR and Recruitment friends: Neil Morrison, John Whelan, Martin Tiplady, Angela O'Connor, Quintin Heath, Val Dale, Adrian Wightman, Peter Cheese, Perry Timms, Martin Tiplady, Julia Rosamond, Paul Jackman, Steve Ingham, Paul Sharpe, Jacky Simmonds, Philip Higgins, Peter Searle, Sam Allen, Juila Robertson, Dan Richards, David Head, Colin Minto, Matt Allder and Mervyn Dinnen.

To my current crew: Cathy Acratopulo, Aaron Aulbury and Emma Leonis at Lace Partners who supported the development of Chapter 10 with their research HR on the offensive. Dave Jenkins and team Wave, Martin Hesketh, Jon Allen, Joe Paget, Cathryn McGinty, Matt Frier, Andrew Fahey of the mighty Brookson, Simon Connington, Rachael Allen, David Shuttleworth, Liam Murray, Ian Saville and Adrian Connington at BPS world. Colin Donnery and Erin Whittle at FRS Recruitment. Christian and Nicola Millam of ExpediteHR. Mark Palmer and Philip Godfrey from OEE. Rinaldo Olivari and Craig McCrum of Coople. Simon King and team JLA – keep the gigs coming. Also to Nicola McQueen and Paul Jezzard – what could have been.

Finally, to my mother Jo and my late father Derek for making me who I am today.

ABOUT THE AUTHOR

Kevin Green has spent close to 40 years in business, the vast majority in leadership roles. He has been an entrepreneur, CEO, MD and Human Resource Director of a FTSE100 business. He now spends his time as a non-executive director and strategy adviser to fast-growth human capital businesses. He is also a TEDx presenter. He believes that developing and helping people realize their potential is an art and a science.

Kevin has either led or been part of top teams who have radically improved performance, growing both revenue and profit, while enhancing the customer experience and developing a people-centred culture. This included leading one of the UK's largest-ever transformations. The outcome was a turnaround which enabled the Royal Mail to go from losing £1.5m every day to making £450m profit in four years while also creating a people-focused culture. He then took a cerebral and dusty professional body and repositioned its membership offering. This included tripling its reserves and being recognized as the best professional body in the UK. He is recognised as a sought-after commentator on the labour market and has been interviewed live by Jeremy Paxman and Evan Davis on *Newsnight* and John Humphrys on Radio 4's *Today* programme. He has also regularly appeared in the *FT, The Times,* the *Sunday Telegraph* and *The Economist.*

01

Why a Competitive People Strategy matters

Introduction

Most businesses are struggling to succeed as their market and industry is disrupted by technology. One reason for this is very few people, deep within businesses, know how what they do every day has an impact on business success. A closer look reveals that most business plans are a mixed bag of tactics that individually might make sense but collectively don't add up to a unified, clear strategy that differentiates the business from its competitors. Most organizations start their strategic analysis by looking at themselves and how they are positioned against their direct competitors. The mindset of many business leaders, often incentivized by share and bonus schemes, is to focus on short-term performance improvement rather than developing a long-term competitive strategy. This mindset often leads to a zero-sum game with short-term tactical developments including cost reduction rather than seeking ways to add more value to current and potential customers.

The world is changing

In the early part of the 21st century it's clear that new industries, products and markets are being created more rapidly than ever before. This innovation is predominantly being driven by new technologies and business models. As Kim and Mauborgne explained in their book *Blue Ocean Strategy*, 'If you find yourself in an ocean of bloody competition with lots of similar competitors all competing on price, you need to extract your business from the combat, so compromise is no longer necessary' (Kim and Mauborgne, 2004). Instead of a red ocean filled with competitors thrashing about in bloody combat they imagined a blue ocean with unlimited demand and high profit. This requires clear choices and trade-offs to be made so you find competitive space where few others are present, and you can make healthy returns. This requires more analysis and thinking about where and how the business should compete.

Customers

To find a unique competitive space or a blue ocean you must start with the customer. The term 'value creation or proposition' is overused but the business that can create huge leaps in value for their customers will always be long-term winners.

If your company lacks a clear, coherent Value Proposition, it won't be focused, its cost structure will tend to be high and its operating model complex. If it can't differentiate its offering from its competitors, and is pursuing a 'me too' strategy, it will find itself in a price war rather than in a competition based on value. When a company isn't listening to its customers, it is likely to be too internally focused with an agenda dominated by incremental internal change. Fast growth companies are often real value innovators where they have spotted latent customer demand and positioned their organization to service this demand. If they aren't providing distinctive customer value, they may just be benefiting from being in a fast-growth industry.

Putting the customer first

Often leaders are told to be brave, entrepreneurial and risk-takers. These all have their place, but data analysis and deep customer insight are proven to help you make better strategic decisions. Looking for customers with un-serviced needs that they didn't even know they had, where a different Value Proposition meets their requirements, is a winning strategy. Think Apple. They have created a vast array of products that customers didn't even know they wanted until they saw and used them. The iPod, iPad and iWatch. This wasn't about more market research; consumers often have little idea of what a new product or service could do for them until it is in front of their eyes. What tomorrow's big winners are doing is looking to develop a product or service that meets untapped demand. One interesting starting point when seeking to think differently about customers is to define who *won't* be the customers for your offering. As Nordstrom and Ridderstråle said in their book *Funky Business*, 'capitalism is simply about creating a temporary monopoly' (Nordstrom and Ridderstråle, 2007). Think Apple's iPad or IKEA. Many competitors have sought to copy or imitate them, but in both cases the innovator has continued to dominate their market.

The link between customers and a Competitive People Strategy (measurement)

These two audiences (customers and employees) are very rarely talked about together, but in reality they should be looked as two sides of the same coin. Businesses are becoming more focused on the wants and needs of customers and potential customers. This is creating wholesale disruption. Let's look at Amazon and how they have disrupted traditional retail or how the internet enabled Apple and Spotify to transform the music industry. Organizations are innovating and seeking to meet customer demands in new ways. Amazon has created a new retail experience where customers order online and get products delivered to their door the next day. In the music industry we can now purchase any piece of music in 30 seconds from our phone; there is no need to visit a shop or wait at home for a CD to arrive.

So a critical starting point of any Competitive People Strategy is to ensure the business has people who can spot potential customer demand

and design new ways of meeting that demand. A commonly held view is that it is entrepreneurs who spot opportunities to exploit. However, in the case of Amazon with Prime, and Apple with iTunes, these were already large established businesses that had no track record in these sectors. Their people identified the opportunity and created a strategy to meet this new demand. This type of disruptive innovation is becoming commonplace. So, an early question when developing your Competitive People Strategy is, do you have a culture, and do you have leaders who ask the right strategic questions of the organization's people? Great ideas don't just belong to leaders. Second, can you bring together teams of talented people to explore and answer the questions about your customer and market opportunities?

Another important part of a Competitive People Strategy is the ongoing feedback process from your customers. It doesn't matter if you measure net promoter score (NPS) or customer satisfaction; it's the direct relationship with your people metrics that is critical. In any service or business-to-consumer organization the ability to deliver great customer service that exceeds the customer's expectation will consistently deliver superior financial results. Many service organizations are rightly obsessed with measuring customer feedback and satisfaction. The use of net promoter scores is providing customer data and insight directly, so your people can see the impact providing a superior customer experience has on how much and how often the customer spends. The evidence is very clear that by measuring and improving your people's engagement, you can make a significant and very positive impact on client and customer satisfaction. The work of Kaplan and Norton on Strategy Maps and the Balanced Scorecard shows the causal correlation between improvements in employee satisfaction and increases in customer loyalty and spend (Kaplan and Norton, 2001). This type of approach also works in non-consumer-facing sectors such as business-to-business, manufacturing and agriculture. It takes longer for the data to feed through, but the causal relationship still works. Therefore, getting your people fully engaged, trained and motivated has a direct impact on business performance, notably on revenue growth and, more importantly, on increased profitability.

Purpose and meaning

A business should be clear about who its customers are and what product or service it is going to provide to them. This business strategy should have a narrative that will explain to shareholders, markets and other stakeholders about how the organization will compete. However, to inspire and engage its people, an essential element of any Competitive People Strategy is a narrative or compelling vision for its people. This vision will create a higher purpose; why we are doing this and why it's important. It won't say 'we are here to deliver superior financial returns for the shareholder'. It will create a sense of purpose for its people, so they know that what they do is important, and why it matters.

I recently worked with a healthcare recruitment business that provide services in the NHS. They were clearly a market leader with fantastic results year after year. They created a focus and a narrative that their customers, candidates and staff bought into. They explained their reason for being as 'helping the NHS save patients' lives'. They described their mission as ensuring the NHS has the right staff at the right time so that if your daughter needs an important operation, your father is admitted to hospital or your partner requires some urgent tests, the NHS has well-qualified, professional staff ready to provide the patient with the medical treatment they need. They went on to say, 'We help the NHS have good-quality, qualified staff at the right time, so patients are put first, operations aren't cancelled, A&E is kept open and tests are always available.' This is a great example of a purpose well described; a narrative that explains why they provide their service rather than just what they do and how they do it. This purpose connects to people's emotions and it places real importance on what their recruiters do each day. The business results of this healthcare recruiter were consistently the best in the industry. They retained great nurses and doctors who chose to only work via this organization. They retain great staff and the NHS Trusts that they work with love them because they show they care about what they do. The by-product of creating a motivating purpose is that staff give discretionary effort. This in turn leads to market leading financial performance that enables the business to keep investing in their people; a virtuous circle.

Jack de Peters, the CEO of Wegmans in the USA, who have consistently been in the top five of the best companies to work for in the USA, said, 'our employees are empowered by our vision to give their best by not letting any customer leave unhappy. We also use our vision to help us make critical decisions and to do the right thing by our people' (Bock, 2015). Therefore, an organization with a Competitive People Strategy has a vision that creates purpose and meaning for the people who work there.

Culture

Any Competitive People Strategy will seek to build competitive advantage through its culture. Culture is 'the way we behave around here'. It's an organization's DNA. Ed Schein, Professor Emeritus of MIT School of Management, said, 'a group's culture can be looked at in three ways' (Schein, 2010); by looking at its artefacts such as physical space and behaviours; by surveying the beliefs and values espoused; or by digging deeper into the underlying assumptions behind these values. However, most think about strong successful cultures based on how employees behave on a day-to-day basis because it's visible – it's the easiest thing to observe. Nevertheless, values are important and the assumptions underneath the values matter even more. An organization's culture brings alive its purpose. If the purpose is 'why we do what we do?', the culture describes how we work together to deliver the purpose. This could be considered as a bit soft and fluffy, but the data shows that strong cultures aligned to a well-defined purpose are far more productive and have better performance as they utilize all their people's skills and capabilities. If people care and believe in what they are doing, they feel it is important, they simply work harder and seek to improve consistently.

Whenever you look at a business that produces great financial results over a long period of time, you will often see a culture that enables them to attract, engage and retain the people they need to be consistently better than their competitors. Culture is the bedrock of an effective Competitive People Strategy.

Teams

In most organizations, teams are becoming ever more important. A Deloitte article in 2016 stated that 'businesses are reinventing themselves to operate as networks of teams to keep pace with the challenges of a fluid, unpredictable world' (McDowell *et al*, 2016). It is also important to recognize that the majority of work gets completed within teams as organizations seek to become both more effective and agile. Sometimes teams are formed to deliver a specific outcome and are then dispersed. It's obvious when looking at how work is currently being organized that more activity is undertaken as projects. It is not uncommon for people to operate in three to four teams at any one time. However, the reason teamwork is addressed in this book is that little time, resource or development is dedicated to helping teams maximize their performance. This is an omission that, if addressed, could help business become more successful, deliver more value and reinforce the organization's culture.

Great teamwork enhances the performance of any organization. In the context of change and disruption it is increasingly difficult for one person (no matter how brilliant or senior) to have the answers to all the organizations problems and dilemmas. Teams by their very nature are made up of different people with different personalities, views, opinion and perspectives. This diversity helps devise and deliver solutions and enables progress to take place. Teams also facilitate learning and development. Team development and effectiveness are underused tools in most people strategies. The focus tends to be on the organization and individuals. However, a deep focus on improving your team's performance is a great opportunity to be better than your competitors.

Leadership

Getting people who have the ability to inspire and engage other people is the core building block of a Competitive People Strategy. Each element of a Competitive People Strategy reinforces the others.

It's an integrated set of interventions that enables businesses to compete. It's not one silver bullet. All the elements need to be deployed in a coherent, systematic and supportive manner for the benefits to be realized. Leaders have a huge impact on organizational, team and individuals' performance. The leadership model we describe later in the book shows how people-centric leaders create a positive work environment. They focus on what creates value for their customer; their people. They, like their peers, will have technical and business skills but, on top of this, they realize that their ability to inspire and motivate others is the key to unleashing their organization's ability to be the best it can. Leaders paint a picture of the future, creating a clear purpose, providing high-quality feedback and acting as a coach and people developer themselves. The organization consistently reinforces that its leaders are accountable for their own, and their team's, performance in a way that nurtures and grows skill and talent.

Followers have very simple expectations of their leaders; they should show they care about their people and that they are open and honest. They also want them to be good communicators and to be able, when needed, to make tough calls and decisions.

Good leaders, according to Jim Collins in his book *Great by Choice* (Collins and Hansen, 2011), figure out what worked and why. They look for data and evidence of what delivers great performance. They are rigorous and disciplined while also being very empathetic. The big question for organizations, and why leadership is one of the six building blocks of a Competitive People Strategy, is how do you attract, and more importantly develop, great people leaders?

If you can systematically build great leadership, you will create empowered, motivated and engaged teams and people.

Employee engagement and experience

Getting people to feel fully engaged in their work is important because the data is very clear – the more engaged a person is the better their performance and productivity. The idea that we can motivate people using a carrot and stick approach has proven to be outdated thinking. There are three fundamental approaches to motivating people at work. You should create autonomy, mastery and purpose. Daniel Pink, in his book *Drive* (2009), proved that organizations that allowed people autonomy to take control of their own work and take decisions about how to get the job done felt accountable, responsible and trusted. Mastery is based on the human desire to keep improving or get better at something. Jobs that allow people to grow and learn improve how people feel about their organization and their job. The third element of improving employee engagement was mentioned earlier in this chapter – purpose, or the sense that people are contributing to something that is meaningful beyond themselves. People want to feel that their work is making a difference or an impact in the world. Engage for Success, the not-for-profit organization leading on employee engagement in the UK, says that only 30 per cent of people are fully engaged at work. If your people strategy can deliver purpose, mastery and autonomy for your people, performance will radically improve as engagement increases. There is a huge opportunity to improve organizational performance.

Another area of focus within your people strategy would be to regularly measure your people's employee experience. This is different from engagement, which is best described as the overall feeling employees have about the organization. The employee experience is a more granular measure of your people's view on everything they experience: technology, work environment, leadership, their manager and HR practices. This enables the organization to get regular data about how the Competitive People Strategy is being executed. Is it leading to an improved employee experience? Getting data on this at regular intervals and at a local level allows you to look for areas of success, so you can learn from them and focus your attention on parts of the organization where an intervention may be necessary. It provides a constant barometer, so you can gauge what's working and what isn't; it's an effective feedback loop.

HR's role

The development of a Competitive People Strategy is not natural territory for most HR functions. However, it provides HR with a once-in-a-lifetime opportunity to move away from being a support function to becoming a creator of value and driver of business success. The majority of time and energy within most HR functions is spent on three things. First, they focus on HR deliverables. They pay people, recruit staff and train people. Second, they create policies or rules for the organization to live by. Third, they ensure compliance to their people policies through procedures and ways of working. This approach to people, while well meaning, is based on two core assumptions. The first is that we need to be explicit about everything to do with people or our managers just won't do it properly. In fact, they will be non-compliant. The second, even more worrying, approach is that we treat managers and staff as being unable to do the right thing unless they are policed. This adult–child approach creates dependence, a lack of confidence and a permission-based culture. This will make the business compliant with employment law and avoid any risk, but it is likely to stifle creativity and innovation, and it certainly won't make the organization a good place to work. Is the HR function the right function to develop and lead a Competitive People Strategy? This is open to debate. The function needs a significant mindset and capability shift if it's going to take on this critical organizational role.

The HR function must move from a defensive, 'let's do good practice or the same as everybody else' approach focused on compliance, policies and procedures, to an offensive or competitive mindset, one focused on 'how do we create more value for customers by encouraging, motivating and inspiring our people to give their best?' This means seeking to work at an organizational level on purpose, culture and leadership development and seeking to define measurable improvements in employee engagement and experience to see if the people strategy is being deployed effectively on the ground.

This is a huge opportunity for the people profession but one also fraught with risk because unless HR can demonstrate their ability to lead the work on the Competitive People Strategy they will be consigned to the delivery of transactional people activity while others such as Strategy or Transformation directors take on this critical role. We are at a tipping point. Can HR up its game and step into its new world? Many have their doubts, but this is a once in a generation opportunity.

In conclusion, businesses are operating in a world that is changing faster than ever before, driven by technology (artificial intelligence (AI), machine learning, the internet of things (IOT) and three-dimensional (3D) printing. Having a strategy of differentiation is becoming more important because a 'me too' organization is fast becoming unsustainable as customers' expectations rise. However, the organizations who look for competitive space by focusing on a unique Customer Value Proposition will be tomorrows winners. To be able to execute their strategy, the winners will also have to deploy a Competitive People Strategy. This is a well thought out approach to all the elements of purpose and culture, leadership, talent, measurement, engagement, great people managers and the ability to lead change and transformation. Those that grasp the opportunity will be hard to compete against as the implementation of a Competitive People Strategy takes time to get right. The people advantage secured is also very difficult to imitate or replicate. A Competitive People Strategy takes time to mature, but if done well it provides long-lasting, competitive advantage.

References

Bock, L (2015) *Work Rules: Insights from inside Google that will transform how you live and lead*, John Murray Publishers

Collins, J and Hansen, MT (2011) *Great By Choice*, Random House Business

Engage for Success (nd) Blogs, research, opinion on employee engagement https://engageforsuccess.org/research-opinion-employee-engagement

Kaplan, RS and Norton, DP (2001) *The Strategy Focused Organization*, Harvard Business School Press

Kim, WC and Mauborge, R (2004) *Blue Ocean Strategy*, Harvard Business Review Press

McDowell, T, Agarwal, D, Miller, D, Okamoto, T and Page, T (2016)
    Organizational design – The rise of teams, Deloitte Insights www2.deloitte.com/
    insights/us/en/focus/human-capital-trends/2016/organizational-models-network-
    of-teams.html
Nordstrom, K and Ridderstråle, J (2007) *Funky Business Forever: How to enjoy
    capitalism*, Financial Times/Prentice Hall
Pink, DH (2009) *Drive: The surprising truth about what motivates us*, Canongate
Schein, EH (2010) *Organizational Culture and Leadership*, John Wiley

02

Strategy – how to compete and win

When talking or presenting to HR audiences around the world, one of the recurring questions I am asked is 'Can good people practice make organizations successful?' My answer is 'No.' It can make them better. It can help them improve, but for any business to be successful it needs to have a clear business strategy and a relentless focus on providing value to its customers.

What has worried me about this question being asked so often is why so many people leaders don't understand the importance of business strategy; and the very idea that doing exactly the same 'good practice' as your competitors is going to give you an advantage is very worrying. Many people leaders have few concepts or tools with which to think about their own business and that of their competitors. HR people just don't spend enough time on understanding how their business competes or what the customer needs they are seeking to address. The issue is two-fold. First, a people strategy not immersed and aligned to the organization's goals won't add much value because it will just be a set of tactical interventions. The business won't have asked and answered the question, 'what do we want our people to do that will help us win.' Second, the HR/people function has a big role to play in business strategy development, which needs to move away from just being about the board and leadership team to a more creative, engaging process that gets ideas from across the organization and unleashes creativity and energy.

Competitive People Strategy

The concept of this book has been bouncing around in my head for years. When talking to business leaders, it is often clear they don't get the importance of people, leadership and culture or the impact it has on the execution of their business strategy, while at the same time many people leaders are in the dark about how their (and other organizations) compete. It's the ability to do both at the same time that makes organizations great, that enables them to compete and win in today's hyper competitive market places. I've worked with many fast-growing businesses over the past decade. While this has been refreshing and energizing, it's just so much easier in a start up to have a clear view of what customers want. However, as an organization grows and matures it often loses its focus and clarity. Size and complexity often get in the way of strategic positioning. Hence a major reason all good people strategy should be ground in the organization's purpose and strategy.

This is a book for leaders

This book has two audiences; the obvious audience is human resources directors (HRDs), chief human resource officers or people directors, or whatever we will call ourselves next. However, it also emerged that CEOs, managing directors (MDs), finance directors and operations directors were as interested in the ideas on culture, measurement, talent and leadership. They are starting to understand the importance of knowledge and intangibles to future business success, but they are struggling to know what levers to pull and how they will evaluate the impact of any investment in people. It's the answer to the same question; how do we compete and win?

Is our job about human potential?

This has become a hot topic of debate over the last five or six years as organizations have sought to become more reactive and agile in response to the disruption being unleashed by technology and new business models. A modern mantra espoused at many HR events is 'let's not forget the people' or 'let's put the human back into HR'. The work that many are doing to make work more meaningful, enjoyable and rewarding is critically important. In fact, many of the concepts they propose are included in this book. The difference with this book is that it's focused on making the business more successful. That's what we are all here to do. Having a people-centric organization that is not successful holds little pleasure. If it's struggling to make a profit, money won't be invested in people, staff start to fear redundancy, cost reduction becomes the mantra and a horrid mixture of uncertainly and relentless pressure creates an environment where values get forgotten and behaviour deteriorates. In this situation, it's impossible, regardless of how good your HR function is, to create a great place to work. Creating a great place to work should support, help and be part of making the organization successful, ie profitable.

The virtuous cycle that we all strive for is when a business is making above average profits. What you find here is an organization that is confident and who has clarity on its customer offering. They have created the ability to invest in the next phase of growth and development. People in this environment are recognized as the creators of value and investment is made in finding talent and making the organization a great place to work. This enables them to continue to be successful. Success breeds success. We all know this, but we don't have a methodology of consistently making this happen. That's why this chapter and the next chapter are focused on the following strategic questions: 'What game are we in and what do we need to do to win?' and 'What could our people do that would radically help us win?'

Your strategy toolkit

When seeking to understand any commercial organization, you have to start by analysing its business strategy. We have identified four tools that business and people leaders should use to explore competitive strategy before they seek to craft or define their people or HR strategy.

Only once the business strategy is fully understood should you seek to describe the human dimension of competitive strategy.

The Five Forces

This is a fantastic tool with which to understand markets and industries, created by Michael Porter, a Strategy Professor from Harvard. His book *Competitive Advantage* (1985) is a seminal text on competitive strategy.

At the core of his thesis was the structural analysis of industries. He says that 'a fundamental determination of firm's profitability is its industry attractiveness' (Porter, 1985). In simple terms, business success isn't just about the business itself, but also the market or industry in which it competes. You must focus first on the market in which the firm competes rather than the business itself. This was revolutionary at the time, but surprisingly is still ignored and misunderstood by many business leaders today. It is clear that a competitive strategy must grow out of a sophisticated understanding of the rules of competition in your own market. To be competitive and successful you must cope with and ideally use the rules in your firm's favour. The Five Forces tool is a way in which you can review and explore all five competitive forces at play in any market. These are: the entry of new competitors; the bargaining power of suppliers; the bargaining power of buyers; the threat of substitutes; and the rivalry amongst existing competitors.

The collective strength of these five competitive forces determines the ability of any firm in that industry to earn a profit on their investment in excess of the cost of capital. This is a great starting point to understand the market or context within which your business competes. It helps teams decide how attractive their market or industry is and to take action based on this detailed knowledge. The strength of the Five Forces varies from industry to industry, market to market. They also change as a market matures and evolves. The critical factor is that most industries are different. They all create different opportunities for firms to generate a profit. In industries where the Five Forces are favourable, such as pharmaceuticals, internet retailers and soft drinks, most of the companies have an ability to earn above average returns. In less attractive industries where pressure from one or more of the forces is very intense, such as steel, traditional retailing and logistics, very few firms will command good returns, regardless of how well the business is run, or how empowered, engaged and motivated the employees are. Always look at an industry first as it often demonstrates that profit is a function not just of how good the business is but also of the market structure itself. The tool is now used extensively to measure competitive intensity, attractiveness and profitability. When used well, it often helps organizations think about innovation and where they can find blue space, where there are gaps, where firms can create new value for customers, that competitors have not yet identified or actioned.

Below is a description of each of the Five Forces. We have identified what each competitive force is and how to recognize its relative force on the competitive landscape in an industry.

1 New entrants

How easy is it for new entrants to start up in your market or industry? The easier (less time and money) it is for a competitor to enter a market and be effective, the more those already operating in this market will have their position significantly weakened. Industries with strong barriers to entry make a market attractive because it's likely that there will be few competitors. Those that invest and survive will make decent returns, but not many will make the business case, raise the finance or bear the long period of losses before making a profit.

2 Power of suppliers

This force addresses how easy it is for suppliers to put up the prices of their products and services. It is affected by the number of suppliers and how easy it would be to switch from one supplier to another supplier. Also, how much would this switch cost? The fewer suppliers and the more a company depends upon a single or a few suppliers, the more power a supplier holds.

3 Power of customers

This deals with the ability of customers to reduce the price they pay over time. It's concerned with how many customers a company has, how much value is derived from each and how much it would cost your customers to switch to a competitor or substitute. The fewer the number of customers, the more powerful the client base, and the more power customers hold, and this increases their ability to negotiate price reductions.

4 Threat of substitutes

Substitutes are products or services that are not the same but could be used as an alternative, and so pose a threat. Think about the growth in the sales of bottled water over the last decade and the rapid growth in coffee shops. They have both had a significant impact on the soft drinks market during this period. If it is easy to bring a substitute to the market at low cost, the number and attractiveness of the substitutes weaken an existing company's power.

5 Competition in the industry

This is often the most commonly used definition of competitiveness. It is the central competitive force, hence why it is placed it in the centre of the Five Forces. This element of the tool looks at the number of direct competitors and their ability to threaten existing firms in a particular market. More competitors with similar products and services lessens the power of the existing business. It also reduces the attractiveness of the industry, as your customers can talk to your competitors if they are unable to get an advantageous deal from you. When competitive rivalry is low, a company has much greater power to increase prices and to grow its sales and profit without changing much else.

The Five Forces determine an industry's profitability because all the forces have a direct impact on price, cost and investment by organizations competing in that market. Supplier power influences the prices a firm can charge, as does the threat of substitution. The power of customers will influence cost and investment because powerful customers can demand much more cost-effective product or services.

Understanding and using Porter's Five Forces to analyse your own industry will enable your business leaders to review their business strategy in the context of their market dynamics so they can take advantage of the industry that they chose to compete in. This is the first perspective that should be used to build a picture of how the business is currently competing and allows your leadership team to explore what it needs to do to take advantage of its market or whether they should be looking at other different market opportunities. In relation to the development of the people strategy, it enables you to define where talent may reside within your market. It may be beneficial to do some People and Employer Value Proposition (EVP) benchmarking of your direct competitors.

Customer Value Proposition

The second tool with which to review your business strategy is Value Propositions. This thinking was developed by Treacy and Wiersema, two Bain consultants who in their book *The Discipline of Market Leaders* concluded that market leading businesses always choose a single 'value discipline' of either best total cost, best product or best total solution and they literally build their organization around their specific proposition (Treacy and Wiersema, 1995). There have been numerous studies that support this thesis. Successful firms that are market leaders excel at the delivery of their proposition to their chosen customers. The key is a tight, laser-like, focus.

Each of the three Value Propositions demands a distinct people strategy and organizational model with its own structure, process, systems and culture. This helps define the areas of focus in relation to people. Operationally excellent organizations are likely to be focusing on improving customer service, workflow and use of the internet to reduce the cost to serve. Product leaders will have a people strategy with a focus on their research and development talent, brand, innovation and marketing capability, while a business with a customer intimacy strategy will be focusing on account management and how to deepen their one-to-one customer relationships.

The three Value Propositions are:

1 **Operational excellence (best total cost)**

Companies that pursue this Value Proposition are not product or service innovators, nor do they cultivate deep one-to-one relationships with their customers. Instead, operationally excellent companies provide middle of the road products or services. However, what they focus on is doing this at the lowest price. Second, they seek to make life easy for the customer; they eliminate inconvenience and complexity. Their proposition to customers is simple – low price and hassle-free service. Think easyJet, Direct Line, WalMart (Asda) or perhaps Lidl or Aldi. These types of organizations have a 'no frills' approach to a mass market. They do what they do incredibly well and consistently by removing complexity and cost while making life as easy for the customer as possible. The internet has facilitated many organizations pursuing this type of strategy. However, in some markets, like logistics, it's become incredibly competitive, with margins under pressure and profitability declining.

2 **Product leadership (best product)**

In companies that pursue this Value Proposition practitioners concentrate on offering products that push performance boundaries. Their proposition to customers is also equally clear – they simply offer the best product in a particular market segment. These types of product companies don't build their propositions with just one innovation; they continue to innovate year after year, product cycle after product cycle. Dyson is a classic case of a product leader in vacuum cleaners, fans and soon to be electrical cars. Nike is a leader in athletic footwear. For these and other product leading companies, competition is not about price. It's about product performance. If the product is the best in the market, then they are free to charge a premium. The people focus will always be on attracting and retaining the core talent that helps with the innovation, such as engineers in Dyson's case, researchers at GSK and new product developers at Nike.

3 Customer intimacy (best total solution)

This Value Proposition focuses not on what a market wants, but on what specific individual customers want. Companies pursuing customer intimacy are not focused on one off transactions; they cultivate meaningful long-term relationships with a high lifetime value. They aim to satisfy unique needs that often only they, by virtue of their close customer relationship, can deliver. These firms will say they have the best solution for each specific customer. They provide all the support needed for the customer to achieve optimum results.

It is worth recognizing that choosing to pursue a Value Proposition is not the same as choosing a strategic goal. The discipline to define and execute a Value Proposition is extensive. It cannot be grafted onto or integrated with an organizations normal operating philosophy. It is not a marketing strategy, a public relations (PR) campaign or a way to promote the company to talent. It's a core strategic decision that shapes all subsequent tactics and plans. This helps people make decisions. You can't have more than one Value Proposition and you can't have elements of each. It's also very difficult, in fact near impossible, to move from one to the other. The landscape is littered with those that have tried and failed. A Value Proposition is how a business choses to compete, how it is different, and how it defines the value it provides to its customers. It also is reinforced by all other leadership decisions being made to support this strategic choice. It colours the entire organization, from its capability to its culture. The choice of Value Proposition in effect defines the broad shape of a company's Competitive People Strategy.

Later in this chapter we will explore management concepts and tools to improve organizational performance, such as Agile and Lean. These are both valuable management tools or approaches that can help businesses get better at what you do. They are powerful concepts that can make a significant difference to performance, but they do not help you define your core strategic Value Proposition. The flaw is that many leaders assume that all that is needed to make the organization more competitive and successful is the deployment of a management tool. The Value Proposition is an effective way to get leadership teams to explore how they compete and what they should focus on and what they shouldn't. Deciding what you are not going to do is still an important strategic decision, which we will apply to people strategy in the next chapter.

If an organization is going to achieve and sustain dominance it must first decide where it will stake its claim, what market it will compete in and what type of value it will provide to its customers. A common mistake is to try to deliver more than one Value Proposition or to adopt operating models best suited to other propositions. Once a business is clear on its market and Value Proposition, it can then decide if the use of Lean or Agile principles would improve or enhance its operating model and performance.

The questions that must always be asked of your leadership teams on strategy and its Value Propositions are as follows:

- What market do we chose to compete in and how attractive is it?
- What does our company do better than anyone else?
- What unique value do we provide to our customers?
- How will we increase this value over time?

If your top team cannot answer these questions easily and arrive at the same answer, then getting this right at the start of your Competitive People Strategy journey is no bad thing. However, as most industries are being disrupted at speed, the value customers expect is being raised daily. Great business leadership starts with deciding which customers you are focused on and how you will provide them with an exciting and outstanding Value Proposition, be it a low-cost offering, a world-class product or a relationship they truly value.

Before you start building a Competitive People Strategy, define and review your market attractiveness using the Five Forces. Next, get your leaders to articulate your Value Proposition and test how good the organization is at executing it.

These are essential tools that will enable your leadership community to go on a shared journey of learning, creating shared understanding and challenging current assumptions. This will throw up tough questions that need decisions. The worst outcome of any strategic review is that the business lacks courage and decides not to make trade-off decisions, and instead fudges the answers. This will not enable a well-thought-through people strategy, but, more importantly, it will lead ultimately to the firm's demise. Being the facilitator of the process enables the people leader to ensure that the big strategic questions are not avoided or ignored and compromises are not made.

The Boston Matrix

The third tool we propose using was designed by the Boston Consulting Group in the 1970s. It is designed to help organizations with their product and service strategy. It assists businesses review their portfolio of products and services. It enables improved decision making on where to invest for profitable growth and potentially which products and services the business should cease providing.

The Boston Matrix works best for organizations with multiple services, products or businesses. Its primary role is to help businesses make better decisions and get the best return by maximizing its portfolio. The matrix is a simple two-by-two, with growth rate on one axis and relative market share on the other (Henderson, 1970).

This results in quadrants, for which specific recommendations apply to each category:

1 **Dog products**
These are products in markets with low growth and where the business has a small market share. The aim here is not to invest any more in these products and services, as they are a drain on resources and are likely never to make significant returns. The organization should seriously consider divesting of business or products in this quadrant or cease providing the product or service over time.

2 **Question mark product or services**
These are products in markets with high growth, but where you have a relatively small market share. As the name suggests, it's not known if they will become stars over time or fall into the

'dog' quadrant. These products and services often require significant investment to enable them to become profitable stars. The challenge for any organization is that heavy investment may be needed to get the required level of return. One recommendation is not to have too many question mark products or services at any one time. Most organizations seek to carry one or two of these types of products.

3 Star products or services

These, as the name suggests, are the best types of products or services to have in your portfolio. They are in high-growth markets where you are either the market leader or have substantial market share. These are the products and services you would be wise to invest in, as the returns on the investment, while not certain, are likely to be significant profit generators.

4 Cash cows

These are the products where the market is mature and there is little market growth. However, because of your strong market share you continue to make good profits. The objective here is to milk these products and services so you can invest in your stars and question marks. Proctor and Gamble has often been described as a cash cow company as its Pampers (nappies) and Lynx (deodorants) products are in very mature markets but they have very high market share and returns continue to be good.

So far, we have provided a set of tools with which any business can explore the market dynamics in which it operates, review its Value Proposition and test its product/service portfolio. The final strategic tool, which has real merit as a way of getting leadership teams to test their strategy and review how they compete, is Simplifying.

Simplify

Simplify, a book by Richard Koch and Greg Lockwood (2016), builds on the two concepts of Value Proposition and the Boston Matrix.

Richard Koch has spent his life trying to identify key principles to business success. He became recognized for his book *The 80/20*

Principle (Koch, 1997). The idea was that the most significant results came from only a small proportion of the effort. However, through applying another principle, which he called the Star Principle, he recognized that real value is created by investing only in stars (Boston Matrix), or those with the biggest market share in fast growth markets.

Yet Koch and Lockwood realized that the best businesses were not just the ones that were market leaders or dominant in fast growth-markets, but those that were also the simplest. They explored how simplifiers like Ingvar Kamprad (IKEA), Herb Kelleher (South West Airlines), and Allen Lane (Penguin Books) achieved such remarkable results over a significant period of time.

They identified two strategies for simplifying: by price and by proposition. The worst proposition for any organization is to be neither a leader in terms of its products or service (what they do) nor a leader in terms of price. Inevitably, competing with neither of these in place means that the business will find itself overtaken and outgunned by firms that focus on one or the other. A company should be either a price simplifier or proposition simplifier to create sustainable competitive advantage that resonates. This is a powerful concept which helps leaders reduce complexity, create clarify and focus on explaining its competitive stance both internally and externally.

- **Price simplifying**
  This involves seeking to drastically reduce the price of the goods or service provided to customers by at least half. It doesn't mean reducing the quality of the goods or service themselves, but rather reorganizing the whole business organization towards greater efficiency, which means a much lower cost for customers. When a product's price is halved, a funny thing happens: demand does not merely double as you might expect, it often increases by fivefold, tenfold or more. Wherever it's been achieved astonishing results have followed. However, the leadership and organizational change required to halve the price of a product should not be underestimated.

- **Proposition simplifying**

  The priority here is 'to make the product or service not just a little better, but better by a large magnitude' (Koch and Lockwood, 2016). This enables it to demonstrably be different from anything else in the market. Not just a little easier to use or a bit more useful, but a significant improvement that the customer can see and experience. People really love great products and services that make their life easier; think Apple's iPad, Google's search engine, and Uber. These products and services usually create a whole new market because they embody pent-up customer demand that was not satisfied because organizations had made the offering either too complex or difficult to use.

Overview

We've not covered these concepts in a huge amount of depth. However, that does not diminish their power to transform how a business competes. We are hoping that readers develop a set of tools with which they can engage leaders and the HR function in thinking about their industry and their customer offering as an important starting point before focusing on people. Second, it is essential to help leaders to understand the importance of business propositions and the segmenting of your offering. A relentless focus on what and how we are seeking to serve our customers is a critical building block in competing through your people.

There is a huge amount of content available on business strategy. However, if you use the four concepts included here you will be incredibly well positioned to assist your organization articulate how it competes. Having applied these concepts to many of the fast-growth companics I am currently working with always encourages new thinking, different conversations, more analysis, better decision making and renewed action. All the businesses have become more focused and developed the ability to communicate their strategy to potential investors, partners and, as importantly, their people, more effectively. They are now very clear on where and how the business competes.

Agile and Lean

Agile and Lean are not strategy concepts but can be used to improve business performance. These are not so much about the business strategy itself, but how you can improve what the business does. They are incredibly helpful tools for people professionals as well as business leaders. Both Agile and Lean can and perhaps should be applied to the HR function itself and the services that it provides.

Agile

It's clear where Agile started – it was an approach used to develop software products. However, the concept is now being used in many different forms within organizations. It's a recognized term for a set of methods and practices that emerged from the information technology (IT) sector. It draws upon other management approaches such as Lean (see next section), Kanban and Learning Organization Theory. It evolved in the software sector to support and improve project management, time management, quality improvement and team performance. At its best, Agile methodology provides a change management and decision-making approach and an extensive toolkit. In its home territory Agile has a manifesto (Agile Manifesto, 2001). Its core principles are that it values:

- individuals and interactions over processes and tools;
- working solutions over comprehensive documentation;
- customer collaboration over contract negotiations;
- responding to change over following a plan.

Most organizations today are seeking to improve or transform themselves due to customer or market pressure. So, it's no surprise Agile has been viewed as a tool that can help achieve this objective.

There is currently a lot of debate about Agile approaches to all areas of management, including HR. It's a good way to think about how to improve the product development process within an organization. HR can use this methodology to improve the development of its products and services, especially the process of co-creating products with line managers and your people.

At the heart of the Agile methodology is learning. It focuses on routine, small incremental improvements with time to report, reflect and learn. Clearly Agile thinking was initially based on the Waterfall model of project management, which involves breaking a complex task into smaller, well-defined projects with a linear flow. This approach is still used as the core methodology for project management but what it doesn't allow for is rework when things need to be revisited and rethought when a team knows the improvement just isn't going to work. So Agile is a way of recognizing that most improvements take more than one attempt to get right and the more we learn about the challenge as we practise improvements, the greater chance that we will find a lasting solution.

Agile has a range of methodologies. Scrum is a management framework that helps to control and manage the interactions and developments within a project. The scrum master is responsible for facilitating the team and its members. The scrum master ensures that sprint planning, stand ups and retrospectives are held, and that feedback is learned from and acted upon. Many of the Agile tools and ways of working can be applied to HR as well as any other parts of the organization. The use of Agile is a very effective method of designing new people policies, processes and procedures. This approach to product development, where proposed people interventions are piloted and tested with managers and employees as users, creates a new dynamic between line managers, your people and the HR function, where it repositions itself as the facilitator or enabler rather than the expert designer. This co-creation process is proven to improve the effective implementation of new products because of testing reflection and learning before organization wide roll-outs.

Lean

Lean is another management approach focused on identifying value creation and improving the processes by which the value is delivered to customers while minimizing resources, time, energy and effort.

Lean thinking and practice help organizations become both more innovative and competitive. Businesses with a Lean mindset see problems as opportunities for learning rather than errors and mistakes to be swept under a carpet. Managers act as coaches, helping teams both identify problems or areas for improvement and facilitate improvement activity on a daily basis.

Lean is not implemented at a macro level. It works best at the level where work gets done. The most famous example of this was Toyota's revolutionary productions system, which was described in the book *The Machine that Changed the World* (Womack *et al*, 2007). Lean is much more than a set of improvement practices; it is a set of behaviours and a management system. It builds superior performance by utilizing problem-solving capabilities of frontline managers and staff. The shared approach of Agile and Lean is that they are people-focused, driven approaches to identifying potential value and then seeking the most effective way of delivery – a service or making the product. A core belief of a Competitive People Strategy is that you need to utilize all the capabilities of your people to help the organization be as good as it can be. The mindset and approaches of both Agile and Lean should be seen as tools and approaches that HR practitioners can utilize to both develop its own people products and to help line managers drive continuous learning as work issues and problems are identified and resolved.

The bridge from business strategy to people

One of the reasons for writing this book was my experience of working with businesses that have a clear competitive strategy but have not created a people strategy that enables them to succeed. A well-crafted people strategy is one of the, if not the, most fundamental building block of any successful organization. It is still commonplace for HR or People Strategies to be a list of people-related activity often decided randomly rather than a set of choices or trade-offs that have been made to ensure the business strategy is implemented and the organization has a purpose, great leadership, a strong culture and seeks to fully engage its people. Great organizations are those that deliver fantastic returns year after year but do this by creating great places to work. They have clear, well-crafted business strategy and a people strategy that is completely aligned. The people strategy defines what specific outcomes the business requires its people to deliver. It is measurable and concise so that it's easy to understand, defines the 'what' and the 'how', and encourages action. Businesses that win over the long term have often found a way to link their competitive drive with how they recruit, train, reward and engage their people. This doesn't happen by accident; it's a rigorous, thoughtful and comprehensive process.

Strategy Maps

My preferred way of explaining strategy and showing its link to people is to develop a Strategy Map. A Strategy Map is a diagram that shows your organization's strategy on a single page. It has a number of powerful features. First, it is a great communication tool. It allows people, wherever they are in the organization, to see how their job affects the achievement of the business's objectives and goals.

The Strategy Map was created by Kaplan and Norton in their second book on Balanced Scores, *The Strategy Focused Organization* (2001). The core concept of a Strategy Map is that each strategic objective is articulated visually and the map shows the linkage between tactical activity so you can view the linkage to the overall business goals. The Strategy Map template has four key elements. At the top is the organization's financial goals, followed by customer objectives, internal processes and then learning and growth. What is powerful is that it demonstrates the relationship between the four different types of objectives. In relation to a Competitive People Strategy it shows how people activity is directly related to the achievement of the organization's strategic aims and goals. It shows strategy in action by showing the relationship between drivers (what we need to focus on and improve) and the desired outcomes. This cause and effect relationship is an effective way to highlight how the strategy will be delivered. This is both a strategy design toolkit and a fantastic communication and involvement tool. It helps businesses design and then manage the implementation of strategic change.

FIGURE 2.1 Example of a Strategy Map

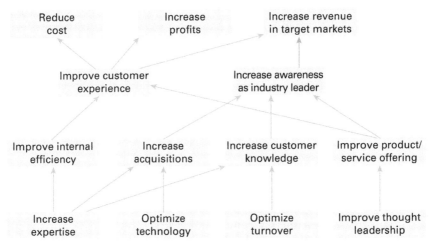

SOURCE Adapted from Kaplan and Norton (2001)

As you can see from Figure 2.1, the Strategy Map also has arrows between objectives to show the cause and effect chain. If you follow the arrows you can see how the objectives in the lower parts of the diagram are what drive the achievement of the objectives in higher parts of the diagram. This clearly demonstrates how great people interventions and development leads to a positive impact on financial results. These causal relationships are critical to a Competitive People Strategy. They show that if you train your employees and build a positive, inclusive culture this will have a positive impact on customer service, and that experience will in turn have a positive impact on customer behaviour and eventually lead to superior financial performance.

This demonstration of the link between people activity as the driver of value creation and effective strategy execution is not clearly understood in many organizations The Strategy Mapping process creates lots of debate, learning and new thinking. The ability to show the business strategy and people strategy on one page with the relationship and impacts clearly defined is a significant tool in the creation of a Competitive People Strategy. This hypothesis, which has been proven in thousands of businesses, shows a measurable relationship between people and organizational performance. It is always about selecting a small number of objectives in each perspective and then choosing measures and targets to track progress. These need to be tested and proven before the final Strategy Map is decided upon. However, a well-formed Strategy Map allows the organization to 'tell a story' from the bottom to top along the lines of 'if we invest in training it will allow us to improve those processes that have a positive impact on customers, who will spend more, and this leads to improved financial results'.

Strategy development as a learning process

The tools explained so far in this chapter could all be used to explore an organization's current strategy and define its competitive approach. The Strategy Map process demonstrates what needs to be driven to deliver the results.

The more creative and engaging the strategic review process is, the more value to the organization. I've seen leadership teams that were trapped in a zero-sum game of ongoing cost reduction transformed by this type of process, which gave them the time and the space to think differently as they went through an engaging strategy development process of reflection and learning.

One of the core attributes and focuses of a great people leader is to develop a creative environment for leaders to think, analyse and come up with new answers to business challenges. There are two worlds in business: the analytical and the creative. Most organizations have both but focus much more heavily on the analytical rather than the creative when working on strategy. The failure to navigate between the traditional world of analysis and the world of innovation not only compromises business growth, it also undermines the ability to create an inclusive culture where everyone is involved in the development of the strategy; where all can contribute regardless of seniority. Strategy should not just be the preserve of the board and leadership away-days. The process of thinking about strategy with leadership teams should be inclusive and more about experimentation and less about planning. We need to think inside out.

My advice to organizations that want to work on strategy is to create an engaging creative process where people are challenged, and new ideas (however random) are explored. Don't rush it; allow the whole leadership population time to think, talk, reflect and engage with others. My experience is that three or four events spread over a three-month period work best. It is also important to get external perspectives during the process. Visiting non-competitive businesses, inviting academics and other business leaders in to talk with and work on the process, adds freshness and different and unique perspectives. These workshops should be away from the workplace and be externally facilitated. They should be a mix of hard process work (using the tools discussed earlier in this chapter) and open space to allow leaders to think differently and creatively.

These types of strategy development processes can, and in my view should, be used with managers and employees across the business. These interactive, participative events can be used to educate and engage while providing insights that encourage the business to think differently about itself.

Conclusion

This chapter has been about making sure the business has fully tested its business strategy; it's looked at the market it operates within. It has reviewed and explored its Customer Value Proposition and its product/service portfolio. It has explored its approach to Price and proposition simplification and decided if it could use Agile and Lean approaches to drive continuous improvement. Once this work has been completed, I propose the development of a Strategy Map, so the causal relationships are shown on a one-page diagram. These are the initial building blocks for the development of a Competitive People Strategy. I also articulated how a people centric strategy development process can help the organization think differently and if used with leaders, managers and employees can create significant commitment from all your people.

BUSINESS STRATEGY CHECKLIST

1 Analyse the dynamics of the market that your business competes in. Reflect on its attractiveness and decide if the business should modify or change its business strategy in light of the forces at play.

2 Use the Value Proposition tool to ensure your leadership team are clear on what value you are seeking to provide to your customers. Then look at your operating model to ensure all activity is specific aligned to your Value Proposition.

3 If you have a range of products or services, then use the Boston Matrix to review and then decide which businesses to invest in and which to divest of over time.

4 Use the Simplify principals of price and proposition simplification as another test of your business strategy.

5 Decide if Agile or Lean could be used to drive performance improvement in your business.

6 Develop a Strategy Map with your leadership population once the other tools have been utilized, to review your strategy. This shows the relationship between people activity, process improvement, customer satisfaction and loyalty and financial results. Keep refining this and testing the causal relationships. This is often the starting point of developing your Competitive People Strategy.

7 Develop a creative, thoughtful and highly participative process for your leadership community to work on strategy. Then roll out the final Strategy Map to all parts of the business as a learning intervention. Seek to modify and improve the map through the process of engagement.

References

Agile Manifesto (2001) https://agilemanifesto.org/

Henderson, BD (1970) *Boston Growth Matrix*, Boston Consulting Group

Kaplan, RS and Norton, DP (2001) *The Strategy Focused Organization*, Harvard Business School Press

Koch, R (1997) *The 80/20 Principle*, Nicholas Brealey Publishing

Koch, R and Lockwood, G (2016) *Simplify*, Piatkus

Porter, M (1985) *Competitive Advantage*, Free Press (Macmillan)

Treacy, M and Wiersema, F (1995) *The Discipline of Market Leaders*, HarperCollins

Womack, JP, Jones, DT and Roos, D (2007) *The Machine That Changed the World*, Simon & Schuster

03

Building a differentiated people strategy

It is still astounding that many, if not most, leadership teams have a limited understanding of the importance of a coherent people strategy to business success. The greatest concern is that in an economy where human capital or people are the foundation of value creation, little new thinking is taking place. It has been shown that up to 80 per cent of business value derives from intangible assets such as brand, relationships, design, intellectual property and an ability to innovate (Skroupa, 2017). This is a leadership dilemma. The asset that is the most important to future business success is the least understood, is very rarely measured and is by far the most difficult to manage.

We are now entering the fourth industrial revolution where AI, machine learning, IOT and 3D printing are disrupting business after business. We are at a tipping point. As new business models ripple through our economies, a new science of people management is needed. In an economy where value creation is dominated by people and the intangible assets they create, there can be no better time to propose a new approach to the human side of business.

In my 35 years of seeking to align people leadership with business strategy, I have come to the conclusion that it's difficult to manage something that we cannot describe or measure. Metrics are the right language to use to describe organizations and strategy. In this chapter we will seek to describe a new framework for developing a Competitive

People Strategy that will deliver superior organizational performance over the long term.

This will enable people leaders to play a more strategic role within their organizations and business leaders to fully utilize their people's potential. In Chapter 2 we explained the importance of Strategy Maps in highlighting the causal relationship between great people management and improved business performance. In this chapter we explore how to use your Strategy Map as a cornerstone or starting point in the development of your organization's Competitive People Strategy.

At the core of a Competitive People Strategy is a belief that only by designing people interventions that make a difference can we demonstrate the link to superior, sustainable business performance. This will not be a comfortable place for many HRDs or chief people officers (CPOs). Designing a people strategy that is evidence based and data-centric means that on occasions we will fail to deliver. In addition, being held accountable for results, not just activity, while not totally new for HR practitioners, will still feel threatening for many. The overriding evidence shows that the vast majority of organizations under-invest in their people or that they invest in the wrong way. So, designing a people strategy with measurement at its heart and totally aligned to business success will enable those who are passionate about people to win the argument once and for all about how investment in people delivers a measurable business return.

The Three Key Questions

Rather than starting with the strategy itself, let's start with a principle. All activity in every business can be represented as a cost. In relation to people activity, we can see and measure the cost (payroll, training and the cost of recruitment) quite easily but measuring the benefit or impact is much more difficult.

The Three Key Questions is one of the simplest and yet most effective tools available to leaders. If you take nothing else away from this book, your money will have been well spent if you apply these three questions. The tool is straightforward; before your business embarks on any new people activity you must ask and answer these three questions:

- Why are we doing this?
- What difference will it make?
- How can we measure it?

If you review your HR strategy using these three questions, a huge amount of activity (up to 75 per cent in my experience) has no clear purpose or measurable objective. This is astonishing; where else within an organization would we allow managers to invest time, money and precious resources without being able to articulate the difference they were intending to make?

Let's look at some typical HR activity. We want to design a new management development programme for managers. We want to change our annual leave policy, or we are keen to use a new assessment tool when hiring. My advice to any HRD or CPO is to send their people away, saying until they can answer the three questions and show the impact, no new investment will take place. This in itself is a huge learning opportunity on how to make data-based or evidence-based decisions. To make decisions in this way, by comparing and making trade-offs based on expected returns, will prioritize the most effective people interventions – those that make the most business impact.

Then why not use the Three Key Questions as a development tool? This would improve decision making and also enable us to evaluate the impact of people interventions more easily. This tool is central to the development of a rigorous people strategy. Any Competitive People Strategy is based on a deliberate set of decisions to create an organization with a clear understanding of what and why it is investing in its people. You can measure this, and you will either succeed or fail. Measurement and defining the impact you intend to make by asking and answering the Three Key Questions are critical in the creation of a Competitive People Strategy.

Capabilities

In the 19th and 20th centuries, financial capital brought advantage because it was a relatively scarce commodity. Technology has since brought competitive advantage because the patents protecting a technology rendered it difficult for others to copy. But financial capital is no longer scarce, and technology is easily imitated today. These resources continue to bring advantage, but they are no longer capable of sustaining the advantage over a long time period. Now it's the ability of your people that will provide sustainable competitive advantage. This is because a people strategy can deliver sustainable long-term competitive advantage if it starts by defining what capability creates value for the customer. Capability can be very difficult to imitate but can make a significant difference to the delivery of your Value Proposition.

Capability advantage

Capability advantage only occurs when your business has a set of skills that are difficult for your competitors to replicate. This is where a unique set of skills, abilities and attitudes come together to create products, services and ways of working that competitors find it tough to copy and compete against. First, it's about recognizing what this capability is and its inherent value to the business. It's also about creating a conducive culture, leadership approach and ways of working that retains the advantage over time. Once you have something unique, how do you leverage or take advantage of it so that it delivers additional revenue or profit growth? The capability that creates improved value for customers is the lifeblood of any successful organization. The ability for financial performance to be explicitly tied to specific capabilities and mindsets is a very powerful part of why defining your core capability is an important part of a people strategy.

Not inimitable

It is also important that the core capability that provides you with a competitive advantage cannot easily be imitated by your competitors, otherwise the advantage will be short lived. This demonstrates that capability is not something that can be easily attracted and hired into an organization. It has as much to do with the culture, development, team behaviour and line manager ability as with the skills of individuals. Here are three different businesses' core capabilities.

- In a leading holiday company, it was its utilization of its airline fleet and occupancy of its hotels that made it the most successful business in its market.

- In a consulting organization it was its account management process and approach that created its advantage.

- In a professional services business it was its ability to leverage technology to remove costs, increase service and make it highly profitable.

In all three situations, the businesses' core capability was not obvious to those looking at it from outside, but internally all three organizations had defined what made them successful and then went about leveraging the ability to even greater commercial success. Once the core capability had been identified, they then established plans to hire, develop and retain the right people, so they could fully capitalize on the advantage they had built.

The measurement challenge

Even in organizations where leaders invest in people, they often question how the HR function contributes directly to business performance. People strategies' influence on a firm's performance remains difficult to measure. However, that's why this is such an essential element of a Competitive People Strategy.

Most people functions focus on the inputs or activity they provide rather than the outputs or outcomes. This is why they find it difficult to demonstrate the impact on organizational performance. The metrics often used, including total compensation, employee turnover, cost per hire and scores in performance management systems, are not tied to specific business outcomes or goals. What we see in most organizations is a disconnect between what is measured and what is important, especially in relation to people strategy. That is why the starting point should be the Three Key Questions and the use of Strategy Maps to search for and find causal relationships between people activity and financial performance.

People as a competitive advantage

The core issue for business leaders and people professionals who are keen to develop a strategy to fully utilize their people is to define their core capability – what set of abilities they possess and their competitors don't. Theses core capabilities should be central to the delivery of the organization's business strategy. By this I mean the capability must be difficult to trade, imitate and secure. Capability is difficult to see and measure, but it is the prime source of sustainable competitive advantage.

What this requires of the people function is a strategic shift from the planning of people activity in the hope that some of it will stick, to a new model of only choosing interventions where the anticipated benefit they are expected to make to the business's performance is clearly defined.

As the focus shifts from utilizing capital and technology to people as the core method of competing, it requires a radical re-think of the notion of capability. People are uniquely different from capital or technology. This uniqueness flows from their very humanness. This new way of thinking about competitiveness requires a deep-rooted reappraisal of how to create a workforce who are fully committed to the organizations purpose and goals; who give discretionary effort and who are fully engaged and committed to doing their best every day.

Organizational capabilities are often the missing link between business strategy and people interventions. They constitute a collection of individual competencies which, when looked at collectively, become organizational capabilities. A great example of core capability was described by Michael Porter in his article 'What is strategy?' for *Harvard Business Review* (1996). Here he defines South West Airline's ability to optimize the number of aircraft in the air by rapidly turning them around on the ground, choosing only one type of aircraft and training staff so they were as productive as possible in the cleaning and refreshing of the planes while on the ground. It's not just the recognition of a core capability that provides a competitive advantage but the organization's ability to fully utilize these capabilities as a central plank of how they compete. This logic assists in the transition between strategy and HR practices. Capabilities serve as the transition from vision and strategy to values and action. As we explored in Chapter 1, as leaders seek to reposition their company with a new business strategy, if they can also articulate the capabilities required to deliver this new strategy, they have a greater chance of executing it. However, two mistakes are often made in relation to strategy and capability. The first is that leaders define a new strategy but don't do anything about refreshing or modernizing the capabilities within the organization. The old capabilities then become a hindrance to the execution of the new strategy.

The second common mistake is the organization defines a new business strategy but then just seeks to put in place the latest management thinking without aligning this activity to the achievement of the new strategy. It's been shown consistently that disconnected management actions, even if they have merit and are well intentioned, do not lead to improvement in business performance. This goes right to the heart of a Competitive People Strategy; it's about ensuring that every people intervention is fully supportive and aligned to the business goals and vision. A congruent and integrated set of people interventions improves decision making, creates clarity of thought, engages employees and enhances the chances of success.

This will often change the organizations internal dialogue from 'How many people have we hired this month?' to the quality of those hires: 'Do we have enough people with the right capability, so we can better serve our customers?'

What capabilities matter most?

The challenge for most leadership teams is that it's likely they will not have spent much time thinking, assessing and testing their organization's capabilities. The starting point is always to see the organization as a set of business processes that serve customers' needs. Core capabilities are the collective knowledge and learning focused on operating these processes across business units, geography and product lines to ensure customers' needs are met. What capability, if you have enough of it, would enable the business to keep winning? It's not just an individual technical skill; it's as much about the structure and ways of working and, more importantly, the delivery of value. When seeking to articulate your core capabilities, ask yourself these three questions:

- First, a core capability should open up market opportunities, not close them down. If it closes down opportunities you've most probably just defined a set of technical skills.
- Second, the value should be defined measured and articulated in terms of customer value. How do your core capabilities provide additional customer value or benefit?
- Third, the capability must be hard for your competitors to replicate or imitate. Otherwise, your advantage will be short-lived and temporary.

Working on capabilities is an essential building block in the process of developing your Competitive People Strategy.

Cause and effect

One of the most powerful outcomes of creating a well-articulated Competitive People Strategy is the narrative or storytelling effect. The company should be crystal clear on its story about how it creates value for its customers. Business can also use Strategy Maps as a way of explicitly describing how people activity will contribute to the firm's success, but, equally important, it shows how the whole system (organization) needs to work in an integrated, coherent way to deliver the best overall performance. At the core is a measurement system that shows how employee behaviour, customer satisfaction and financial performance are all linked. What Sears (the US retailer) did was move beyond a hypothetical model and devise a specific methodology to demonstrate objectively people's contribution to the implementation of the company's new strategy. They got to a defined formula:

- 5 point improvement in employee attitudes DROVE
- 1.3 point improvement in customer satisfaction DROVE
- 0.5 per cent improvement in revenue growth.

(Kruse, 2012)

To achieve great alignment between business objectives and work on processes, customers and people, a company must engage in a two-step process. First, business leaders have to fully understand how value is created by the firm. Second, once this narrative is fully understood, they can then design the correct measurement system.

The business must look beyond the financials, which are the outcome of a well-executed business strategy, to what drives superior performance. To truly grasp the value creation story, a business needs to identify its performance drivers (such as customer loyalty). In addition to that, it needs to define the causal flow or the linkage between performance drivers and financial results. An example of this was a retail client who could measure the impact of a new colleague induction programme. The introduction of the new on-boarding process improved checkout efficiency (customers served per hour) and increased customer satisfaction from shoppers who had asked staff for product or product location questions. Both of these measures could be shown to positively impact on business performance as spend per shop visit and repeat purchases increased following the introduction of the new induction programme. Leaders need to test this flow and causal relationship so that they can explain it internally to their people and externally to shareholders and customers. This helps others within the organization to start to appreciate and understand what creates value. Figure 3.1 shows the basic causal logic that encourages organizations to focus just on what drives value.

FIGURE 3.1 Value creation

SOURCE Adapted from Kaplan and Norton (2001)

Measures need to be defined for each part of the value creation process. This then enables causation to be measured and improvement activity to be tested to see what will deliver the most customer and business benefit.

Grasping the relationship between key success factors is essential for measuring people's elusive role in driving organizational performance. Once a firm has anchored its people activity and metrics in its strategy implementation system, it can then see the connection between what the people do every day and the results the company achieves. The core to getting this right is to recognize the relationship of tangible and intangible assets and of financial and non-financial measures. The complex value-generating connections among a firm's customers, operations, people and technology are often surprising, as is the way organizations integrate and align the activity.

It is also important to recognize the important distinction between Lagging and Leading Indicators. Lagging Indicators such as financial measures, typically reflect only what happened in the past. These metrics show you the impact of earlier management decisions. However, apart from learning about what worked in the past, they don't help you run the business more effectively nor make better decisions. Therefore, you also need a set of metrics that are Leading Indicators. This will be different for each firm, but an example might include research and development cycle time, customer satisfaction or employee engagement. These are the indicators that should be focused on once you have proved that their improvement has a material impact on the firm's business strategy and results. They are future orientated rather than past focused.

The most famous example of taking this logic and implementing it consistently was Sears in the 1980s. They have since struggled, like most retailers, because of the 'Amazon effect', but by using the customer service–profit chain, they became the world's most successful retailer for well over a decade. Let's start with the results achieved. In a 12-month period, Sears employee satisfaction rose by 5 per cent and, as a consequence, its customer satisfaction improved by 1.3 per cent. These don't seem like big numbers, but these improvements led to $200 million in additional customer revenue. Their market capitalization grew significantly as a result. The business was worth 25 per cent more as a direct consequence of the implementation of their initial causal model, which they called the employee–customer service profit chain (Rucci *et al*, 1998).

This consisted of creating links between three components:

1 Making Sears 'a compelling place to work', with, for example, support for ideas and innovations, and employee growth and development (measured through metrics including employee satisfaction).

2 Making Sears 'a compelling place to shop' through offering excellent customer service and high-quality products at an affordable price (measured by customer satisfaction and retention etc).

3 Making Sears 'a compelling place to invest' via revenue growth and efficient asset management.

Visually, a customer service–profit chain can be represented as shown in Figure 3.2.

FIGURE 3.2   The customer service–profit chain

Employee satisfaction	Customer service	Customer loyalty and spend	Superior financial results

Other key users of the customer service–profit chain include the coffee shop Starbucks and Enterprise Car Hire.

At Starbucks they worked out the additional value generated from increased store visits and customer loyalty from improved customer satisfaction. The difference was that satisfied customers would make twice as many visits per month and be loyal for 8.3 years, whereas an unsatisfied customer would only be loyal for just over one year and visit much less frequently (Moon and Quelch, 2004). The impact of twice as many visits over a seven-year period had a huge positive impact on revenue and even more on profit.

With Enterprise Car Hire, it became clear that 'completely satisfied' customers were over three times more likely to rent a car again than 'somewhat satisfied' customers (Taylor, 2002). This led to an extensive training programme and a customer service overhaul because the impact on the business's profitability was so significant.

In both examples, improvements in customer satisfaction were driven by a relentless focus on customer service, including training, changes to the employee reward programmes and progression, based on its customer satisfaction survey. These people interventions were used to demonstrate to staff the critical impact their performance had on customer perception, and both revenue and profit growth. This enabled both businesses to be explicit about what they were seeking to achieve. It enabled them to measure how well it was being implemented, identify what else they could do and get the frontline people fired up to provide great service every day. They had proved beyond doubt that their jobs mattered.

Developing your Competitive People Strategy

The development of a Competitive People Strategy can be achieved by following a six-step process with a focus on both core capabilities and the causal relationship between your people, customers and business performance (see Figure 3.3 on page 53).

Step 1: Clearly defined strategy

Firstly, as explained in Chapter 1, business strategy should be about exploration. What market do you operate in? How attractive a market is it? What pressures are at play? These are just some of the questions that need to be asked and answered. This will enable a clear view of the organization's Value Proposition and its product/service portfolio. Out of this comes an articulation of how the firm intends to compete and what is important in the implementation of that strategy.

Clarifying your organization's strategy, having made relevant trade-offs is not always easy and often takes time and practice. The key thing is to recognize that the company's goals must be easy to communicate and engage your people. If your employees understand what is expected of them and what great looks like, and if they also know that their job performance will be measured, discretionary effort will improve. The linkage between individual, team and organizational performance is a significant starting point.

Step 2: Create a Strategy Map

As explained earlier, I am a great advocate for developing a Strategy Map as a key method of articulating how the strategy will be implemented. The Strategy Map describes the firm's customer value chain and the relationship between key business activities. The customer service–profit chain and the relationship between people, operations, customer metrics and their impact of financial outcomes can be shown in the form of a Strategy Map. In Chapter 2 we defined a competitive and inclusive approach to strategy development. I believe that the top three levels of leadership within an organization should be involved in the development of the Strategy Map. The diagram and mapping process should involve leaders and managers from across the organization. This not only improves the quality of the

Strategy Map, but also increases people's commitment. The questions that are often thrashed out during the strategy development process include:

- What strategic goals and outcomes are critical rather than nice to have?
- What are the drivers for each goal?
- How do you propose to make progress on each of these drivers?
- What are the barriers to achievement of each goal?
- How would your people need to behave to ensure that the company achieves these goals?
- What capability would we need to achieve these drivers?
- What should we change to help us achieve these goals?

The data collection process can be intensive, and I propose that information-gathering tools including questionnaires and focus groups are used to test people's thinking and understanding of what will make the organization successful. This needs to happen at a granular level so that the hypothesis can be tested and piloted. The Strategy Map can take several months and many iterations to complete. Once you think you have a draft picture of your firm's value chain, translate this into a conceptual model using simple language and a Strategy Map. This diagram can then be used to test the initial hypothesis. Testing the thinking with people throughout the firm and, towards the end of the process, with customers, suppliers and stakeholders, throws up lots of improvement opportunities. Organizations that use the Strategy Map externally get an objective viewpoint that is a very powerful way of validating and testing their thinking. Customers, suppliers and stakeholders all like to participate.

Sears and Starbucks are good examples of companies that fully tested their hypothesis and further refined their Strategy Maps based on actual data and evidence. Sears used the metrics initially identified, but they got better at seeing the causal relationships and so enhanced the quality of their whole measurement system, which in turn enabled them only to focus on an activity that made a difference to customer behaviour, and ultimately to business results.

Step 3(a): Identify people deliverables

In the Strategy Map, your people drivers and enablers will obviously become apparent. My advice is to always focus on the kinds of strategic behaviours that can be measured and are directly related to your business results. In the Starbucks example, aligning people satisfaction with that of the three customer metrics described in Figure 3.2 enabled them to see the relationship between great employee behaviour and the impact it had on Starbucks customers. A recruitment business that I worked with implemented a customer service–profit chain focused on improving how their consultants scored their team leader. It was only once they had been doing this for six months that they realized the teams giving great feedback about their leader outsold the other teams by 50 per cent. The recruitment business then realized the power of frontline managers and that their ability to give feedback, coach and motivate consultants was the biggest factor in driving revenue and profit growth. Hence, the focus on looking at the difference between average and good people management became a huge organization performance driver and something that is now reviewed on a monthly basis, with improvement plans seen as a critical business focus.

Step 3(b): Assess the organization against the Competitive People Strategy building blocks

The drivers of great performance and people engagement are the core elements of a Competitive People Strategy. At the end of each chapter in this book we have created a checklist. The questions included there should be asked of your organization as part of the people strategy development process. If the wider leadership team feel the organization needs to invest more in improving its leadership capability, culture, talent acquisition, engagement or change capability then, again, a direct causal relationship should be sought, tested and validated so that the planned activity can be integrated into the Strategy Implementation System.

Step 3(c): Define your core competitive capability

As part of the people strategy process, use the questions in this chapter to work with your organization's leaders in defining the essential core capability that enables the firm to successfully execute its business strategy. Test the quantity and capacity required to achieve the organization's goals and define your current stock. If there is a gap, this becomes a priority acquisition strategy to address in the people strategy.

Step 4: Articulated Competitive People Strategy

This should be the culmination of the strategy development process, Strategy Map, building block review and capability mapping. It will define the areas for investment in people. However, it will also articulate the proposed impact it will have on the organization's performance. All significant people activity will have metrics defined so that a return on investment can be measured and used as the basis for organizational learning. People strategies should have no more than five major strategic thrusts that, if delivered upon, will go a long way towards the achievement of the firm's business strategy.

A highly effective people strategy will fail if it's not constantly tested for alignment to the business objectives, and if it's not periodically reshaped to remain relevant. Misalignment between people strategy and business objectives destroys value very quickly.

Step 5: Define people measurement

This can be integrated as part of the people strategy itself, but the final step in the development of a Competitive People Strategy process is to ensure you can measure each element's potential impact in order that effective implementation can be reviewed. This is where all the core metrics established for each part of the strategy are reviewed to ensure the correct measures have been chosen, andthat there is a causal relationship to the business' goals and objectives. The metrics should be a mixture of financial and non-financial and should be representative of

FIGURE 3.3 Developing a Competitive People Strategy

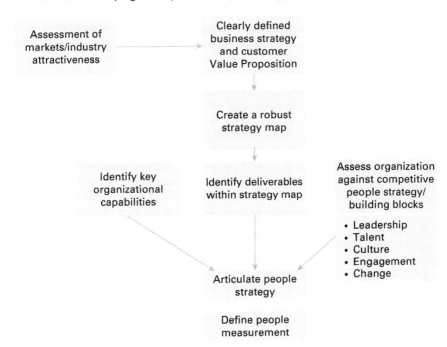

the customer value chain. Clearly, measuring people interventions on the firm's performance is not an all-or-nothing proposition. Progress beyond traditional transaction measurement approaches will, over time, yield substantial improvement later in the value chain. The more sophisticated the measurement system, the greater the eventual business benefits.

COMPETITIVE PEOPLE STRATEGY CHECKLIST

1 Review your current people strategy using the three key questions. Only allow activity to stay in the people strategy if you can answer all three questions. How much activity remains in your current HR/people plan? 25 per cent? 50 per cent? 75 per cent?

2 Describe your organization's core capabilities. How easy or difficult has this been?

3 Describe your organizations internal value chain and relationship between people activity and overall organizational performance in a Strategy Map.

4 Test your Strategy Map by looking for customer service–profit chain causal relationships between people activity and overall organizational performance.

5 Test your people metrics versus the potential impact on business performance. Could you make a return on investment case for the people strategy?

6 Once you have developed your initial strategy with your wider leadership population, seek both customer and supplier feedback.

7 Develop a Competitive People Strategy for the business with four or five major thrusts and define core measures that can be used to evaluate progress towards successful implementation for each strategic thrust.

References

Bock, L (2015) *Work Rules: Insights from inside Google that will transform how you live and lead*, John Murray

Bourdreau, J and Lawler, EE (2017) How to measure HR effectiveness, *Talent Economy*, October

Denning, S (2016) HBR's embrace of agile, *Forbes*

Gratton, L (2000) *Living Strategy Putting People at the Heart of Corporate Purpose*, Financial Times/Prentice Hall

Heskell, JL, Jones, TO, Loveman, GW, Earl Sasser, W and Schlesinger, LA (2008) Putting the service–profit chain to work, *Harvard Business Review*

Johnson, M (2000) *Winning the People Wars: Talent and the battle for human capital*, Times/ Prentice Hall

Kaplan, RS and Norton, DP (2001) *The Strategy Focused Organization: How balanced scorecard companies thrive in the new business environment*, Harvard Business School Publishing

Kruse, K (2012) Why Employee Engagement? Forbes www.forbes.com/sites/kevinkruse/2012/09/04/why-employee-engagement/#66f015a73aab

Mayo, A (201) *Human Value of the Enterprise: Valuing people as assets – monitoring, managing measuring*, Nicholas Brealey

Meritocracy (2017) How to measure HR metrics, Meritocracy blog

Michaels, E, Handfield-Jones, H and Axelrod, B (2001) *The War for Talent*, Harvard Business School Press

Moon, Y and Quelch, J (2004) Starbucks: Delivering customer service, *Harvard Business School Review*, February

Pfefter, J (1998) *The Human Equation: Building profits by putting people first*, Harvard Business School Press

Porter, ME (1996) What is strategy? *Harvard Business Review*

Rucci, AJ, Kim, SP and Quinn, RT (1998) The employee – customer – profit chain at Sears, *Harvard Business Review*, February

Skroupa, CP (2017) How intangible assets are affecting company value in the stock market, Forbes www.forbes.com/sites/christopherskroupa/2017/11/01/how-intangible-assets-are-affecting-company-value-in-the-stock-market/#2ae84f1a2b8e

Taylor, A (2002) Driving customer satisfaction, *Harvard Business Review* https://hbr.org/2002/07/driving-customer-satisfaction

Ulrich, D (1998) *Delivering Results: A new mandate for human resource professionals*, Harvard Business Review Series

04

Leaders everywhere

At times of change, when organizations have to respond to market disruption and the consequent reinvention, business leaders who can inspire, motivate and engage their people are critically important. Hence why leadership is one of the key drives of a Competitive People Strategy.

While great leadership used to be the focus of those just at the top of organizations, it is now required more pervasively within businesses. It's apparent when looking at successful organizations that more change requires higher quality and more rounded leaders to help departments, functions, teams and individuals not just cope with change but to embrace it, flourish and thrive.

Historic leadership models

When we think about leadership many of us immediately reach for the military concept, which has a clearly defined model of command and control. This was adapted in the early 19th century to a mechanistic view of organizations as the industrial revolution took hold. While market, customer, employee and stakeholder expectations have grown, our thinking about leadership has not evolved from this view of a 'leader as hero' model. In fact, our thoughts about leaders have remained pretty much constant over the last hundred years.

This 'leader as hero' and top-down approach needs to be modernized in the face of the challenges businesses face in today's environment.

The current market upheaval is consistently exposing poor leadership; think BHS, Toys R Us, Ted Baker and Sports Direct. Many organizations have been unable to redefine, readjust or modify their strategy in light of the market or technological disruption that is now prevalent, because of a lack of leadership capability to lead the reinvention.

Companies that have been sustainable and successful frequently have leaders that understand that it is people who create wealth and growth and transform how the business competes. Great leaders unleash their people's ability and enable creativity and innovation to flourish while also securing greater discretionary effect from the people in the organization.

The magic combination

Having worked in or with organizations for around 40 years, it's clear to me that the leaders that succeed often have two traits: personal humility and intense professional will. This is very different from previous generations of leaders, who majored on direction, instruction and control. Today, leaders need the ability to continuously listen and learn while providing solutions to business and market challenges. This is a big ask, one without precedent. Leaders don't need to know all the answers, as they did in previous eras with less change to cope with. Today, they need the confidence to admit they don't know all the answers, but know the right questions to ask of the organization. Today's leaders must create the right environment where their people are prepared to challenge and question the organization's assumptions, including how the business competes. This humility, the willingness to admit you don't know all the answers and to be authentic, requires inner confidence, resilience as well as an open and engaging manner. However, this also needs to be combined with the strength of character to make tough decisions, and the critical ability to see the bigger picture. Being an effective communicator is as important as explaining the business vision and purpose to their people; it's an important leadership task.

Leaders in a VUCA world

The reason why leadership is such an important element of a Competitive People Strategy is that the environment in which our businesses operate is being transformed around us. One model that describes this dynamic is VUCA. VUCA stands for volatility (rapid large-scale change), uncertainty (unclear about present and future outcomes), complexity (many factors to consider with no single cause or solution) and ambiguity (lack of clarity on what events mean and their potential impact).

The term was originally coined by the US military after the Cold War and helped their understanding of the disruptive and different forces at work. It also highlights that leaders must recognize that they need to operate differently to their predecessors as markets are disrupted and organizations seek to become more agile and responsive to survive.

The VUCA model highlights both the threats and opportunities for organizations to consider. This model is incredibly helpful to leaders who are seeking to lead their business and thrive in the modern world when more businesses die, and new ones are created every day. This turbulence will only accelerate as AI, machine-learning and IOT become more widespread. The leaders of tomorrow are going to have to be comfortable with uncertainty, ambiguity, complexity and velocity,

FIGURE 4.1 Leading in a VUCA world

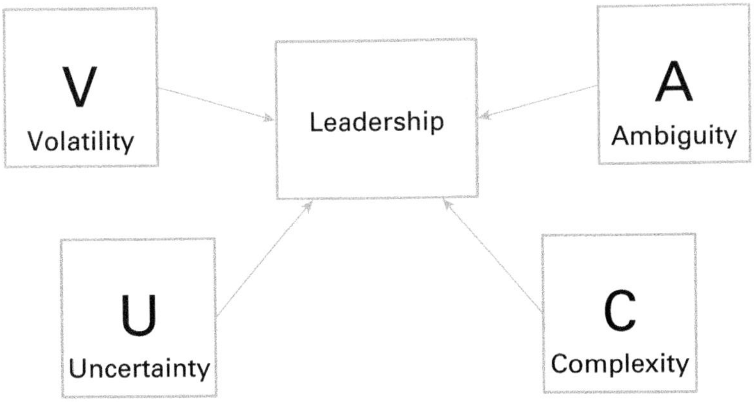

as organizations will have to become better at learning, reflecting and adapting to this radically changing environment.

The five things great leaders do every day

The need for leadership has never been more apparent. However, businesses find attracting, retaining and developing leaders, at the volume required, an increasingly difficult task. The demands are greater and our expectations increasing. This section explains the five attributes of highly effective leaders. Having effective modern leaders who possess these five attributes will assist the business attract high-quality people to the organization.

1. They paint a picture

Great leaders have ability to create a sense of purpose and energy within an organization. As constant transformation becomes a near norm, the ability to set a destination becomes ever more business critical. This needs to be balanced with an ability to create a compelling narrative that excites and inspires people, so they give greater discretionary effort. In times of change people seek certainty and look to their leaders to define where the organization is heading and explain why what the company does is important.

Good leaders ask questions of themselves, their fellow leaders and the organization before making critical decisions. The ability to analyse markets, customer behaviour, competitive pressures and technological advances so that the right questions get answered is essential. This builds trust and openness within the organization. People want to be listened to and have an opportunity to challenge the firm's assumptions. However, organizations can't slow down while engaging their people. Creating clarity of purpose and defining a journey allows workers to provide ideas, be creative and innovate. Great leaders often like to communicate, listen and engage directly with their people, to explain the business strategy, to encourage new ideas and to seek feedback. Effective leaders are ambitious for the organization. They are always seeking improvement and looking for their managers and people to find new ways of working and providing greater customer value. However, they also need to be rigorous, with milestones being defined, goals agreed, and accountability delegated so that the business is executed effectively and the organization doesn't become just a talking shop.

2. They are able to find good people

Talented and effective people who are critical to a business's success are attracted to enterprises that are recognized as possessing strong, encouraging leaders. You will notice the term 'brightest people' wasn't used. Finding talented people who can put their ego to one side and contribute without looking for personal recognition is difficult. Effective leaders spend significant amounts of their time on finding the right people to help lead and manage the organization. They also understand that developing future leaders is an essential part of creating a sustainable business. They do this by focusing on succession planning and performance management, both of which should involve meaningful feedback. Making sure that the right people are on board is a central part of any leader's role and a key component of a Competitive People Strategy. A good leader focuses on developing more leaders, not creating more followers. Organizations that invest significantly in developing and growing their future leaders will have an advantage in the long term as talent and skill becomes more difficult to attract and hire. The ability to fill leadership roles from within rather than having to buy it in from the market with all the inherent risk involved makes an effective contribution to a consistent, inclusive culture. Leaders are becoming more aware of their own bias and are working hard to avoid only hiring and promoting people in their own image. The data on diversity is clear that teams that are diverse and have people from different backgrounds, be that race, gender or sexual orientation, consistently outperform those that are not. The quest is for leaders with the required hard skills plus humility and human attributes. This means that firms should seek more balanced and diverse teams, even if this takes considerably more time. The benefits and results are compelling; finding good people from all parts of our society has to be the right course to pursue. It does require leaders to find new ways to attract, promote and retain good people. This is a major area of impact for chairs, CEOs, MDs and leadership teams collectively.

3. They create great teams

It is widely acknowledged that any task is better performed by a team than an individual. No one individual, however talented, will make as good a decision as a diverse, well-led team. The ability to bring together different abilities, mindsets and competencies is a core leadership trait that needs to be nurtured. Any top team should role model the behaviour expected across the organization, including spending time, energy and effort on the people agenda. However, today teams are often brought together for short periods of time to focus on the achievement of one task. Some people work on many cross-functional project teams at the same time, sometimes across continents, time zones and functions. This necessitates a new leadership approach to team composition, development and communication. This again reinforces the need for leaders to be able to form high-performing teams at speed. Again, this emphasizes why leadership capability needs to be widely disbursed across businesses.

4. They champion a culture of learning

Leaders who will thrive recognize that one of their most important roles is the promotion and facilitation of learning. They champion this for individuals, teams and the organization as a way of improving performance based on data evidence and insight. At an organizational level, it is about adapting to a turbulent environment with rapidly changing customer demands. They personally provide constructive feedback so that individuals learn while doing. They also know that people and teams seeking to stretch and improve themselves will on occasion fail. The leader's role is to ensure that learning can be taken from all work experiences. The avoidance of blame is critical to creating a business that learns, and which is agile and responsive. One of the key organizational attributes of successful business today is to 'fail fast', ie pilot products or services, build on those that work and eliminate those that don't. Leaders who create a culture of continuous learning and improvement based on metrics, feedback and insight are building effective business response mechanism in as fast-changing environment.

5. They are authentic learners

Leadership is a critical organizational capability. It's a fundamental part of all successful people strategies. What is very apparent is that employees want their leaders to be real people. The idea of a leader as a heroic loner does not resonate with employees. They want their leaders to be rounded people, to be able to show vulnerability, be humble, to be idealistic, to have values and demonstrate empathy. This can't be underestimated. Leaders need to show they live in the real world and can empathize with people inside and outside the organization. This creates a relationship with the firm's employees that enables them to feel comfortable in following. Perhaps this is the biggest mindset shift of today's leaders; they are open, approachable and can reflect, seek feedback and recognize they can also improve. This vulnerability to be your true self, to admit mistakes, is an important component of people wanting to work for leaders who demonstrate this type of inclusive leadership style.

Leaders with duality

The leadership element of developing a robust people strategy is intrinsic. When working with leadership teams, I've often asked them to score themselves and their leaders against the indicators shown in Figure 4.2.

What's important about these indicators is that most leaders feel more comfortable with one set of indicators than the other. They are naturally either more people-centric or driven. However, the ability to be a good leader is enhanced by one's versatility to move across the

FIGURE 4.2 Leadership indicators

People-centric		Driven
Openness	vs	Ambitious
Vulnerability	vs	Determination
Long-term	vs	Short-term
Idealist	vs	Pragmatic
Compassionate	vs	Relentless for improvement
Storyteller	vs	Data-savvy
Reflect	vs	Lead fast

indicators and be able to work on both sides of each spectrum. The best leaders utilize both sets of behaviours at the same time, to deal with different situations. Leadership is totally context specific and the aptitude to move between long- and short-term thinking or creating a great narrative while also interrogating data, is essential. Leaders who develop the competence to use all these approaches have a wonderful array of situational responses. They have a fully developed leadership tool kit, so they can adopt the right leadership approach for any given situation.

Competitive leadership

The traditional linear and time-based approach of leadership development is no longer fit for purpose. We need new ways of developing the leaders that will be able to steer firms through turbulent waters. The idea that you join a company as a graduate and go through a slow, prescriptive development programme as you slowly rise through the ranks until you achieve a leadership role is both old fashioned and ineffective. However, many large organizations are still developing leaders in the same way as they did 30 or 40 years ago! This won't work for aspirational leaders, who are demanding real time feedback and the opportunity to learn while leading. The development of leaders should move to a more people-centric approach that builds on the concepts explained here; that people are the drivers of improved competitiveness. This mindset shift is required not just in our businesses but also in the wider education system and specifically our business schools. We need to reinvent leadership development so that it is more experimental. This requires both a new dynamic and systematic change to how we teach young people in schools, colleges, universities and business schools.

In the following section we review some of the concepts that should be included in any leadership programme being developed by an organization.

Fast learners

Speed is now everything, or close to everything. The talent that joins any business has a choice about where they work, and all the data shows that learning, development and progress are the key elements of both attracting and retaining leadership talent. Young leaders are hungry to understand how great people management can lead to improvements in performance and productivity. Millennials and Generation Z want to grow, develop, learn and progress quickly. There is an impatience that needs to be recognized. They seem to want to experience leadership opportunities and accountability much earlier in their careers than previous generations. So, our systems for both hiring and developing potential and proven leaders needs to be more responsive, dynamic and transparent. Leaders expect commitments to be achieved and honoured.

Progressive organizations will also seek to provide learning opportunities for all their employees throughout their working life as they want to keep their workforce fresh, updated and energized. The idea that you do your learning early in your career and then just apply the same approaches throughout the remainder of your working life is now laughable. We need to create a great learning experience for our leaders, so they get the opportunity to learn from outside the business. One way of doing this is to create a mentoring programme. This can be supplemented by coaching and formal training interventions, perhaps all at the same time. We need to create new programmes based on real life experiences to develop leaders at pace.

Problem-centred leaders

Organizations are seeking more of these non-traditional leaders as work becomes more entrepreneurial and project based. A different type of leader is emerging. I call them 'problem-centred leaders'. They do not naturally identify themselves with top management. They will, if pushed, describe themselves as a project manager or coordinator. This is a learned pattern of behaviour and is very similar to that of entrepreneurs in a start-up business. Often the founder has this type of attitude, attributes and leadership style. They often don't like traditional organizational leadership, which they see as boring, task-focused and bureaucratic. What motivates them is solving a difficult problem. This problem-solving style of leadership rarely gets taught, and if it does, it's not called 'leadership'. Yet there is no denying that these types of problem-centred leaders achieve great things; they get stuff done. More large organizations are recognizing the need to hire and retain creative problem-solving leaders across their organization.

These leaders don't behave or look like old-school leaders. They know what they are good at and don't want to be viewed as a traditional manager or leader. They often don't expect people to follow them in the traditional sense, as they don't see themselves as charismatic. They may lack status and aren't great at budgeting or resource allocation. They also, importantly, don't want a traditional leadership career. They just want to get important stuff done. However, what's so powerful about problem-centred leaders is they get others excited about the problem they are seeking to solve. Having fallen in love with an issue, they step up to leadership as a consequence of resolving the problem.

This type of entrepreneurial leadership is an intermittent activity, as people with enthusiasm and expertise step up to solve a specific problem and then step aside when the project is completed. Rather than being pure leadership generalists, or careerists, these individuals pursue their own deep expertise. They expect to be involved in initiatives, which means establishing teams and then disassembling them when the task has been achieved.

A key attribute of this problem-led leader is building a team at pace. They will be good at finding the right talent and convincing others that it's worth getting involved. If there is no interesting problem to solve, these types of problem-led leaders will often go freelance, start their own business or jump ship to another organization that they perceive to have something worth doing. Whenever you meet these types of leaders, they don't describe themselves as a leader, they will just talk about the work they like doing. 'I just want to solve an issue, and that seems to get others motivated to get involved.'

For me, organizations that are being disrupted by new entrants, whether technology or the need to innovate, should go all-out to hire and retain these new entrepreneurial leaders. These types of leaders are critical, yet in many businesses they are often ignored or, at best, accommodated. However, they should be sought out and developed for the great contribution they can make, even if they never want to be on a formal leadership team.

Leaders who don't just engage, but inspire

When you look at consistently high-performing teams or organizations, you will find leaders who don't just communicate and engage people, they inspire! While leadership is context-specific, the organizations that consistently sustain success over many years or even decades often find leaders who can create a culture of inspiration. The capability to inspire is partly driven by an ability to create a compelling narrative and release energy by empowering people and giving them autonomy over their own work.

Inspirational leaders also seek to build on people's strengths rather than fixing weaknesses. This is consistent with research into leadership. According to Gallup, the market research company, the odds of employees being engaged are 70 per cent when the organization's leadership focuses on the strengths of its employees, compared to only 9 per cent when they focus on fixing weaknesses (Rath and Conchie, 2008). Recent research by the strategy consultants Bain shows that the single most important attribute of an inspirational leader, as identified by employees, was centredness (Garton, 2017), which was described as a state of mindfulness. It was described as important because it improves one's ability to stay level-headed, cope with stress, empathize with others and listen more deeply.

As the nature of work changes and today's employees are looking for so much more than just a salary, leaders who inspire and who can help create an inclusive learning culture are ever more important. Talented people have a choice about where they work, and so inspirational leaders are critical in attracting and retaining value-enhancing talent to their organizations.

A leadership toolkit

In this section we explore some of the tools that have been used by successful organizations to hire leaders and those with the potential to become effective leaders. We explore how to improve your selection of leaders, as the interview alone is such a poor predictor of leadership competence. We also define how to get serious about succession planning and the development of leaders.

Recruiting leaders and potential leaders

First, define the leadership ability that would be essential in delivering your business strategy, but be sure that you consider the five leadership attributes described earlier in this chapter:

1 They can paint a picture, they can articulate a compelling narrative that people relate to and feel inspired by. Test their ability to do this as part of the hiring process. In addition, ask them to do a role play presentation explaining the business strategy to a set of new starters. Was this inspirational? Did they pick out the emotional as well as the logical to communicate?

2 They find good people. Ask them about their track record of hiring/ finding great people. Review the strength of their current team. Look for a track record of them developing leaders who have gone on to bigger and better roles. Do they have a track record as spotters and developers of talent? Test this by asking them to explain in detail the teams and development process they used to grow people in their team.

3 Ask them to explain how they built a great leadership team. What was their process? Explore their views on the practice of team leadership. Again, as part of the selection process, ask them to role play a team leadership situation where they led a team in solving a real work-based problem. Ask for their feedback at the end of the exercise, to test how reflective they are.

4 Explore how they develop their people. Don't forget, the best leaders are great coaches and teachers. When assessing for potential leaders, give them case studies of individuals, some of whom are not performing and others who are excellent performers. Allow them time to prepare and then observe them giving feedback and creating development scenarios.

5 Authenticity. During interviews ask candidates to explain mistakes, failures and times when they have felt uncomfortable. Explore their ability to reflect about themselves and how much learning they gained from each situation. How comfortable are they in their own skin? Also, use psychometric tests to provide useful insight into their leadership personality.

The hiring process

We have known for many years that interviews are not effective or reliable selection tools. Studies at major companies including Google have found that interviews are very poor at predicting ultimate job performance (Bryant, 2013). They are even worse at evaluating leadership potential, the ability to inspire, provide feedback, listen to and solve problems. So as part of your Competitive People Strategy make sure you build assessment and selection processes that improve the likelihood that you will only hire leaders who have got the attributes, skills and competencies described earlier.

Whether it's for a leadership role or a potential leadership role (graduate/young manager programme), ensure these two approaches to selection are included in your hiring strategy and you are likely to radically improve the probability of hiring the right leaders:

- **Collaborative hiring**
  Involve a range of people in the assessment activity – some as observers of assessment activities, others as interviewers and some having informal conversations. Ideally, involve the prospective peers and team members of the role being selected for, people who would work for the individual if appointed. If possible, include others from functions that interface with the role holder. In some cases, involving external parties such as customers or suppliers for (for example) account management roles is very helpful and informative. Utilizing a range of people with differing roles and perspectives allows for a diverse set of values to be taken into account. Additionally, this helps to counter any unconscious bias during the process. The more people involved in the selection process (within reason), the more likely an organization will make better and more robust hiring decisions. This mitigates the risk of making a wrong hire, with the additional cost and impact on productivity and performance.

- **Provide a real work assessment or test**
  Create exercises or selection tests that are as close as possible to the real job activity the post-holder would be expected to undertake if appointed. Make any assessment activity as realistic as possible. Engage the staff who would be involved in the process for real in the selection process, either by role playing or observing all the candidates during the assessment exercise. The validity of subsequent hiring decisions is improved significantly if real job tasks have been included in the selection process.

These two processes are proven to improve an organization's selection process for leaders and potential leaders. The cost of getting hiring decisions wrong is expensive. A recent Recruitment and Employment Confederation research report (2017) identified that the cost of a wrong hire in a managerial role being paid £42,000 per year was £132,000, or over 3.2 times the salary. In a bigger leadership role, the cost would be substantially higher.

Succession planning

If your leadership development process is working, you should have at least two high-quality internal candidates for every leadership role that becomes vacant. The strength of your leadership pipeline is a critical part of any people strategy. Have you been investing in your leadership potential so that you have the ability to fill the majority of senior roles internally with top-notch candidates? Only 57 per cent of employers have implemented plans to ensure that there is a pool of leaders and managers who are appropriately skilled to fill future vacancies (ILM, 2012). A formal and regular process should be undertaken, with the top team taking time to consider and review the capability and bench strength of their leadership population. This should happen at least twice yearly and involve a deep dive into every leadership role and the identification of potential successors. The process is often more robust if external expertise is used to provide objective, impartial input to the review. This enables more specific and tailored leadership development to be put in place for individuals identified as having leadership potential but who are not quite ready. It also enables you to identify real areas of weakness, so you can either do some speculative external hiring or start to develop new external talent pipelines. The data for these formal succession planning sessions need robustness and should include performance review data, business results, people and customer satisfaction scores, 360 degree feedback, plus some level of external objectivity around leadership potential.

Leadership development

Most businesses spend a significant amount of time and effort providing strategic, technical and business development for potential leaders. This is a good thing, although it is questionable whether the development provided will be good enough to develop the quality and volume of leadership capability required for organizations in the next decade.

First, any potential leader needs robust and regular assessment. For potential leaders identified in your succession plan, we propose rigorous feedback from both internal and external sources. An external coach to develop new approaches to business and people issues is also a good investment. The assessment should involve 360 degree feedback from peers, stakeholders and direct reports yearly (at a minimum) and ideally every six months. They should also undertake personality and psychometric tests so that their behaviour and self-perception can be reviewed in the assessment process. The feedback should focus on strengths more than weaknesses and provide time and space for potential leaders to challenge themselves and explore their drives on a regular basis. The coach should be chosen by the individual from a pool selected for their expertise and ability by the organization. This ensures that they have the skills required and a good understanding of the business requirements. The coaching should focus on personal drives, results delivery as well as behaviour and personal development. In addition to an external coach, supporting potential or young leaders with a mentor provides them with access to someone who has held senior leadership roles themselves and is prepared to listen, advise and strategize with the mentee.

However, these are just the traditional formal development interventions. It is clear from research that potential leaders need early opportunities to learn while doing. Most CEOs and HRDs would acknowledge the risk of appointing potential leaders into real leadership roles. This should not be underestimated. It can be mitigated by ensuring informal leadership opportunities have been utilized first, such as managing a project team or covering for someone who is on sick leave, maternity leave or secondment. This allows the organization to have seen them lead people and deliver specific tasks before giving them their first proper leadership role. You don't learn to drive a car by just passing the theory test; it's the practical 'doing it' for real that matters most. They will need support and encouragement both internally and externally, but opportunities to lead teams, achieve results and fail on occasions are all part of developing effective leaders.

A new leadership development process that looks like it has merit is leadership labs, where people are taken away from their real job for an immersion programme. This may be just for a week or slightly longer. They are given real problems to solve and a team of people to help them achieve their task. The whole process is filmed and observed. This provides real feedback about how they handled the team, the task and each individual. This has been viewed as a way of speeding up leadership learning without any significant organizational risk. They are costly but are beginning to be seen as a highly effective development tool for those who show early signs of potential.

Secondments have fallen out of fashion, but the opportunity to work in a different environment or context is often hugely rewarding and a great development opportunity. However, these need to be well managed and the feedback should be well constructed so that the learning is captured, shared and acted upon.

Coaching and mentoring should not only be used for young or potential leaders, as transformation and change are now the order of the day for all leaders, whatever their stage of development. It seems only logical to provide real time external input and leadership advice during the whole of your leader's career.

PERSONAL REFLECTIONS OF BEING AN MD, HRD AND CEO

For me, leadership has always felt natural. At school and in sports teams, I often found myself being picked or selected as captain. I was a good club runner in my late teens and early twenties. During this eight-year period I had three different but all excellent coaches. The experience of defining goals at the start of each athletics season, training hard under the watchful eye of my coach who would provide advice, guidance and feedback, was, I think, significant in me becoming a leader. It taught me you need to set strategy goals, you need to measure progress, get feedback from someone who is in your corner but will give it to you straight. You need to work hard to get better and you are the only one who can achieve your goal. No one else can do it for you.

Having left school, I then found myself managing both my athletics club and my Sunday football team. As my career progressed, I asked myself why this was. I think I had some natural attributes: I liked being accountable, making decisions and testing myself. I was always good at communicating and connecting with people and was not afraid to provide feedback and ask people to learn or work harder for the team. However, when I asked team mates why they wanted me as their captain or manager, they said two things which surprised me. The first was that I showed I really cared about what we were doing, and second, I was prepared to try new things both strategically and tactically.

At 29 I was made MD of the consulting organization QTAB. I have to say that in the first couple of years there were as many failures as successes, but I learned from them both. I worked with a coach (no surprise there) who got me to look at myself in detail. I sought out experienced people to act as mentors and non-executives, and I listened to those that worked in the business. I had a great partner in Sue Higgins, who had complimentary skills to me and was also an effective leader. We grew the business; it became successful with many household brands as clients, and as well as running the business I had the golden opportunity to work with the leadership teams of our clients. I observed what worked and what didn't, and I sought to influence, coach and advise, many times successfully.

After 12 years of leadership I decided to join Royal Mail PLC, which was losing £1.5 million a day (BBC News, 2005). I joined first as the Chief Learning Officer and latterly as the Human Resources Director for the letters business, which had a £7.5 billion turnover and 200,000 people. I worked with and observed recognized leaders as they grappled with one of the biggest turnarounds in UK corporate history (see Chapter 8). Following this experience, I became the CEO of the Recruitment and Employment Confederation (REC), the professional body for the recruitment industry in the United Kingdom. I was appointed Vice President of our global body, the World Employment Confederation (WEC). These were small organizations; the REC had 80 staff when I arrived, but we were representing, and I was leading, a £35.5 billion industry in the United Kingdom. In my time at the REC we had to reinvent ourselves at least twice and survive the worst recession in living memory. My four chairs at the REC were excellent sounding boards, and I would consider all of them friends even though there were a few disagreements along the way.

So, from my personal career as a leader, what have I learned about the role? The first thing to say is that it's a team game; you must create a leadership team with a shared agenda, work ethic and no egos. A great CEO or MD can't do it on their own. They have to create a functioning, competent team who are all prepared to put the business before their own career aspirations.

Spend time with your team and others in the firm exploring and thinking about how the business competes. Define a strategy and involve your people in the process; get ideas from everywhere, challenge and talk honestly and directly to the people, whether it's a business of 200,000 or 20 people. Once the strategy is clear, set goals, milestones and metrics at all levels. Hold people to account. Performance always matters. Spend a good percentage of your time talking to and communicating with your people.

Spend time on hiring great people. Don't rush this. While skills are important, make your decision based on their values and their fit within the business culture and team ethos. My worst mistakes have always been when I've listened to my head rather than my heart on people decisions.

Recognize that change is more than sticking values up on the wall; it's about changing how work actually gets done. Customers are king; bring them into the business, get them into the business, get them to provide feedback and spend time really listening to what they have to tell you. They often give you the answers you were looking for. At the REC, I would tell the team when we got feedback we didn't like and just before we got defensive, 'They pay our wages.'

In all, it's been a blast. I've learned a huge amount about human nature and as much, if not more, about myself. Leadership is fantastic and painful at the same time. It's rewarding and disappointing. It can make your head soar but it can also be frustration and lonely. However, it's something worth doing well, it's important and it matters.

In the last year I have become an advisor and non-executive. I've enjoyed helping leaders of many medium-sized businesses find their own way of leading their organization. There is never 'one way' of leading. In any people strategy, getting the leadership bit right early on is essential.

Conclusion

Leadership is an essential component of a Competitive People Strategy. Finding people who can articulate a clear purpose and vision, create an engaging narrative and who recognize that it's the people who create value in the organization is critical, and such people are hard to find. Attracting individuals with the attributes we have described is becoming more difficult. The risk of hiring from outside the business is profound, with a significant degree of uncertainty. Firms need to up their game and invest more thought, resources and time into leadership development. The thinking, development and retention of leaders who are humble, authentic and empathetic while also being commercial and strategic is one of the core challenges of any progressive people strategy. Leadership is the first pillar, as without it much of the rest of the proposed approach will be ignored. The leaders who pursue a people-centric business and a long-term strategy will avoid creating companies that are poor places to work, that fail their customers on the altar of short-term profit and are excessively rewarded before performance deteriorates and they are called to account.

Leadership is the hardest job in business; it frequently demands long hours, lots of time away from home and having to make decisions that affect others' lives. We need to develop our people to do these roles at a rate like never before. It is now essential.

LEADERSHIP CHECKLIST

1 Recognize the importance of authentic, inclusive and empathetic leadership to your organization. Challenge the traditional top-down 'leader as hero' thinking.

2 Incorporate the changing external environmental (VUCA) model into your leadership development and hiring process.

3 Use the five leadership attributes to test your selection, retention and development of leaders and potential organizational leaders.

4 Integrate the duality model as part of your leadership development activity.

5 Recognize that leaders want to learn and progress at pace. Ensure you assessment, feedback and development processes can do this.

6 Identify any problem-centred leaders as part of your succession process and find ways to retain and fully utilize this leadership ability.

7 Review your recruitment processes for leaders. Ensure the assessment and selection involves testing candidates and using the collaborative hiring concepts.

8 Develop your leadership succession planning so that it becomes a critical people strategic activity, twice yearly.

9 Review and amend your approach to leadership development so that it involves the different processes recommended, including coaching, mentoring, 360 degree feedback and leadership labs.

References

Bain and Company (2018) Bain Inspirational Leadership System

BBC News (2005) Royal Mail delivers record profit, 17 May http://news.bbc.co.uk/1/hi/business/4553933.stm

Bryant, A (2013) In head-hunting, big data may not be such a big deal, *New York Times* www.nytimes.com/2013/06/20/business/in-head-hunting-big-data-may-not-be-such-a-big-deal.html?_r=1&

Buckingham, M and Coffman, C (1999) *First Break all the Rules: What the world's greatest managers do differently*, Simon and Schuster

Dawes, D and Petersen (2013) Belief in the unstructured interview: The persistence of an illusion, *Judgment and Decision Making*, 8 (5), pp 512–20

Garton, E (2017) How to be an inspiring leader, *Harvard Business Review* https://hbr.org/2017/04/how-to-be-an-inspiring-leader

Gino, FA (2019) *Rebel Talent: Why it pays to break the rules at work and in life*, Pan

ILM (2012) The Leadership and Management Talent Pipeline www.tvwleadershipacademy.nhs.uk/sites/default/files/11.%20Leadership%20%26%20Management%20Talent%20Pipeline%20%28ILM%202012%29.pdf

Nisbett, R (2015) Why job interviews are pointless, *Guardian*, 22 November

Rath, T and Conchie, B (2008) *Strengths Based Leadership*, Gallup Press

Recruitment and Employment Confederation (2017) *Perfect Match: Making the right hire and the cost of getting it wrong*, REC

Rosen, RH (1997) Learning to lead. In *The Organization of the Future*, Jossey-Bass/Drucker Foundation Series

Tichy, NM with Cardwell, N (2002) *The Cycle of Leadership: How great leaders teach their companies to win*, HarperCollins

Walker, S (2017) *The Captain Class: The hidden force that creates the world's greatest teams*, Penguin

Willingham, D (2103) Why interviews don't work, *Washington Post*, October

05

Developing a winning culture

Why do 87 per cent of people say they are not engaged at work? (Gallup). We know that when people are engaged in their work they are happier, more productive and don't change jobs. All leaders want their organization to be a great place to work because they know it has an impact on the business's performance. We know culture matters, but few organizations know how to review their culture, and even fewer know how to modify or change their organizational culture. This is a critical component in a Competitive People Strategy, as achieving a more inclusive and engaging culture is proven to lead to improved business performance.

Let's start with busting a myth. In my 40 years of working on the people side of business, people have often equated a great culture with having fun. I believe work is work. It's where we turn up to get stuff done. If you look at organizations with winning cultures (those that win awards like Great Places to Work), it's not the 'bells and whistles' (the football tables and office games) that employees value. It's about how people are treated on a day-to-day basis. It's the organization living its values that make a difference. Does your organization define, communicate and, more importantly, live its values? Do you use your values to help you decide who to recruit or who gets a pay rise or who is fired? I think fun is the outcome of a coherent, well-defined set of values that are lived every day and help the business succeed by meeting or exceeding their customers' expectation. Now that's a great culture! So, fun should not be the target; it's a by-product or outcome of a great organizational culture.

When thinking about culture, recognize that every organization has a culture even if it's never been defined. A good starting point is to ask yourself 'Do we have a core purpose?' Can we answer the question 'Why does this business exist?' or 'Who are we seeking to serve and how will we know if it's successful?' The follow-up question in relation to culture is 'How do your people behave when no one is watching them?' The core of winning culture is people working together in a consistent manner to achieve a shared objective.

Different types of culture

In 1994 James Baron and Michael Hannan, two professors from Stanford University, started a longitudinal study into what creates an environment of trust within a firm. They sought to explore the relationship between superior business performance (profitability) and how the organization treated its workers (Baron and Hannan, 2002). The professors were both trained sociologists and so took an academic approach to their work. They studied over 200 technology firms that were in the start-up phase. They did this to observe the companies' culture as they developed over time. They tested and explored lots of activities that they thought might contribute to a firm's culture; these included the recruitment process, who was selected (and on what basis), HR practices, how staff were rewarded and the approach to downsizing and redundancy.

Their conclusion was that there were five predominant ways to describe the cultures that they observed. The data that supported these were based on three criteria:

- attachment, or how strong the emotional bond was between the organization and workers;
- selection – how people were hired (not so much the process, but on what basis: skills, fit with culture or potential);
- control and co-ordination – how much autonomy and freedom people got in their work, and how much bureaucracy was involved in the organization.

The five types of culture were described thus:

- **Star Model**
  In these firms, talent was hired from elite universities or recognized, successful brands. However, they were always looking for potential star performers. They gave their employees huge amounts of autonomy. The offices were often impressive, with pinball machines and cafes. They paid top wages and provided a significant amount of resources to the people they hired.

- **Bureaucratic Model**
  These organizations provide challenging work opportunities to develop. They selected staff based on their qualifications and skills. They had job descriptions, project planning processes and formalized control of working.

- **Engineering Model**
  These firms were very project orientated. Again, selection was based very much on skill and qualifications. They went further and defined specific task abilities for each role. Think of a Silicon Valley, Skunk Works mentality.

- **Autocratic Model**
  These companies were very focused on monetary reward and viewed this alone as their driver of motivation. They were very controlling environments with close personal oversight. Selection was based on a very high adherence to job/task skills. The overriding premise was 'you work, you get paid'. The businesses were often dominated by the founder or CEO.

- **Commitment Model**
  These organizations were very focused on the emotional buy-in of their employees. Selection was based on cultural fit. They were the kind of business where peer support and coaching were in evidence. 'CEOs in these organizations often believe that getting the culture right is more important than having the best product,' said Baron.

Performance of the different models

Baron and Hannan were unprepared for what they found when they revisited the companies towards the end of the decade-long study.

The Commitment Model delivered the best results over time on every single performance measure, including profitability ratios. They were also the fastest to go public (float) and tended to have leaner structures, with fewer middle managers than many of the other models. This is because if you choose your employees in a thoughtful way, over time, you hire people who thrive in a self-directed workplace. These firms had fewer policies and were very focused on delivering for the customer. They also had far fewer personal agendas. Many venture capitalists commented that these firms were more resilient, as the initial growth was steady and it allowed the business to establish a way of working that was values led. The Commitment Model outperformed every other type of management approach in every meaningful way. 'Not one of the Commitment firms studied, failed,' said Baron.

How to build a commitment culture

There seem to be some consistent messages to leaders who want a culture that delivers great results but at the same time want to create a business where there is a sense of trust amongst workers, managers and even customers. These types of cultures encourage people to work hard and to give a bit more effort. They also stick together when times are tough; every business, regardless of its culture, has set-backs. We know from Gallup's research that businesses that have engaged people are 22 per cent more profitable than those with employees who are not giving their all (Sorenson, 2013).

There are five essential building blocks to creating a strong, commitment-based culture:

1 Create a clear, coherent purpose statement – why we do what we do and why it's important. This needs to stand the test of time.

2 Define, embed and live the 'values'. These need to be real so that everyone uses them every day to make decisions.

3 Hire and develop 'authentic leaders' and have 'people managers' who can coach (Chapter 3 and Chapter 9).

4 When recruiting talent, don't get obsessed with superstars. Make sure people 'fit the culture' and are team players (Chapter 6).

5 To improve work performance, use development tools that engage your people in co-creating the solutions, such as Lean and Agile (Chapter 2).

In the rest of this chapter, and throughout the rest of this book, we explore how to establish the building blocks of creating a competitively successful culture where trust is high, and people give their best and feel empowered and motivated to succeed.

Purpose: Start with why

Having worked with hundreds of organizations over the last 35 years, it is apparent to me that many have not defined, or even know, why they exist. Simon Sinek, in his famous TED Talk, said that most companies know what they do and how they do it, but the 'why' is often missing (Sinek, 2009a). The majority of people at work can easily describe the product or service the company sells. Most employees can also describe what they do personally and how this helps the company do what it does. The 'what' is easy to identify. Once you've got a 'what' some organizations go further and define 'how' they do what they do. This often describes how the business competes; it may involve a specific process or something that enables the firm to have a unique selling proposition. 'Hows' often describe how the business is better than or different from its competitors. This is an advancement on the 'what', but while it is important, does it provide enough to fully engage your people? Does it help to make your company a great place to work? In his book *Getting to Why* Simon Sinek says it's the '"Why" that very few firms can articulate' but it's the 'why' that creates the emotional buy-in and attachment (Sinek, 2009b). Why do they do what they do? So, defining your 'why' means explaining your fundamental purpose. Why does the business exist? What is it that helps people get out of bed each morning, turn up, care about what they do and, more importantly, give their best?

To develop this approach, you need to think inside out, whereas most organizations communicate from the outside in. That's because it's so much easier to talk about 'what' you do. It is a lot easier than answering the 'why' question. Most firms are happy to talk about 'what' they do, and some go further and define how they go about doing it, but very rarely do they define' why' they do what they do. This is the initial process in starting to develop a commitment culture.

Knowing your 'why' is not the only way to be successful, but it is the only way to maintain a lasting, sustainable competitive advantage. Often, organizations lose a sense of their original purpose as they grow and expand, for example. This stretch leads to them becoming fuzzy, with no one sure 'why' they are doing what they do anymore. Consequently, it becomes much more difficult to maintain growth, and both customer and employee loyalty. The initial inspiration that drove the business's original success has been forgotten or lost and so the business just keeps repeating what it's always done. Hence, as customer habits change, the business is at risk of being left behind.

Therefore, when starting to explore culture, start by asking your people, customers and suppliers 'Why do you think we do what we do?' If you keep getting answers to this 'why' question that are really answers to the 'what' and 'how' questions, then you should get serious and set about articulating your 'why' so your businesses has a clear purpose.

Seek your people's input every day

All great commitment cultures have a second trait, in addition to a clear articulated purpose; it's that people are trusted to make decisions about their own work. They are also encouraged to contribute ideas on how to improve the business and the customer's experience. If you believe people are inherently good, then organizations should find ways to seek their people's input about how the organization delivers on its purpose. Google's former HRD, Laszlo Bock, said 'You need to give people slightly more trust, freedom and authority than you are comfortable giving them. If you are not nervous, you haven't given them enough' (Bock, 2015). People often look at the physical work environment as a way of understanding a business culture because it's the most visible. However, it's the values, and the assumptions behind those values, that really matter.

Real values

Organizations that have succeeded in creating a great culture do not just articulate the values and the behaviour they expect. They go further; they use the values to continually test or challenge the businesses systems, processes and decision making. The businesses values need to make a difference to how the work gets done. I've observed hundreds of organizations who have defined their values; they have hung them up on the wall and put them on screen savers, but when I've asked their people about them they don't remember what they are, let alone know if they are used as a cornerstone of decision making. We've always known that employees pay more attention to what really happens, the action that's taken, than what's said or written on the walls. Actions always have, and always will, speak louder than words.

Embedding values

A great way to think about values is that they shape how the work within an organization gets done. If personality influences the behaviour of an individual, shared assumptions about what is valued by any business influence opinions, attitudes, behaviours and, ultimately, the business outcomes.

It's no surprise that what really makes a difference to how employees experience the culture of an organization on a day-to-day basis is their relationship with their manager and colleagues. Values that really stick and make a difference are those that are reinforced by the following leadership behaviours:

- Leaders treat everyone as an individual but deploy the same behaviour with every person. Managers live and use the values every day. This reinforces fairness.

- Leaders create a climate where everyone has a voice, so ideas and suggestions are sought from all. This encourages people to feel they belong and are listened to.

- Business leaders use the values to communicate why they have made decisions so there is a level of transparency that encourages openness and dialogue.

- All parts of the organization have the same levels of autonomy and decision making. People want to feel that the values are used consistently across the organization.

- Information is openly shared with all employees wherever possible, good and bad. Everyone is treated as adults and given as much data and information as is possible. This should include data on how the business is performing and the plans the business has to improve. Leaders constantly ask for feedback from everyone on the business' plans.

Defining your values

I've been in many rooms with leadership teams intent on creating a new set of values for their organization. While this is a worthwhile exercise at the beginning and the end of a cultural development process, it won't be effective if it's the whole process. Values cannot be imposed from above; they need to be owned and co-created with people from across the organization. If it's an inclusive and comprehensive process it will deliver something meaningful to the workers and the leaders of the business. If you don't involve your people, customers and suppliers in the process you may well end up with a set of value, despite your good intentions, that feel like they were plucked from a generic 'all purpose' list of virtues, including 'integrity, excellence, respect, customer centric and efficient'. Let's be honest, every decent business should espouse and live those! These are describing what every business should do, not what makes you unique or different. What you are seeking to define is what makes your organization win consistently. This is not an easy process; you need to dig deep, spend time on it and make sure it is ground in reality and not a motherhood and apple pie statement that no one can argue with. You must keep going back to the 'why' question. Your purpose is where the passion resides and why the organization was created in the first place. What customer needs are you answering? Jack Welch, the ex-CEO of GE, said that a good set of values 'are so real they smack you in the face with their concreteness' (Welch, 2005).

The value creation process must touch everyone in the business. They should have something to say, they have a stake in the outcome. Creating values is an iterative process; it takes time. Yes, it will be messy, but if it's going to be used to describe how the company behaves then it's important that it is as good as it can be. In small organizations you can get everyone in a room for two days and come up with something to be proud of. In larger organizations it's tougher, but you still have to engage the people, use meetings, training sessions, team away-days, surveys, idea events, social media and internal communication tools like Slack to get your people's input. Creating real participation and getting views from everywhere makes a big difference to the quality of the values. However, more importantly, it creates greater buy-in, commitment to and belief in the final set of values. Don't forget to involve other stakeholders, customers, suppliers and partners close to the business towards the end of the process; use them to sense-check the outcome. Getting them to kick the tyres and provide feedback from their own perspective creates a robustness and rigour which again helps to ensure you have created something that will stand the test of time. My advice is, use the values for as long as possible before revisiting them.

Values matter most when they are tested

Living your values should be uncomfortable at times. It holds you to a set of behaviours that in certain situations, leaders, HR and even your employees will want you to compromise on, for example when the business is making an important decision. It could be around how you make more money or the desire to hire someone who some are not convinced will live the values but who has some expertise that the business could really use at that moment. This is going to sound very black and white, but values are not soft; companies should recognize and reward those who exhibit the organization's values and punish those who don't. I never thought I would use the word 'punish' in my people strategy book! For example, asking someone to leave your organization even though they are highly competent and loved by your customers because they don't like the values, will create noise and reaction from other staff and managers. This is when you have to explain that the values are not about some people following them and others not; they are how we work together. They are non-negotiable. This is when values matter, when they are used to help you make a tough call. It's no accident that this chapter follows the one on 'leadership'!

Culture: Over-managed and under-led

To develop a commitment culture, you need to role model the organization's values consistently. In many, perhaps even most, organizations people are over-managed and under-led. Many of you will have interviewed hundreds of people over the years. You know that no one, when asked how they ideally want to be managed, has said, 'I want to be micro-managed, to be told exactly what to do for every minute of the day'! There may be people who go to work and don't want to think or make any decisions, but why would you ever want to employ them? If you don't want your people to think then why not automate the work by programming a computer that can learn while doing (machine learning), do it more efficiently (make fewer mistakes), not take holidays and deliver 24/7. The routine jobs, even the cognitive ones, are in the process of being eliminated from organizations at warp speed. To retain and engage your people while this change is occurring requires a culture of inclusivity and participation. The humans you want in greater numbers than ever before are those that think, create and add value. The saying 'with every pair of hands you get a free brain' captures this well, and it is the leader's job to put employees' brains to work as well as their hands.

The theory of management is based on an outdated view of what motivates people at work. The theory was that humans are motivated at work by reward or punishment. The theory went along the lines of 'if we promise to raise your pay, you will work harder. If you delivered the project to time and budget, you will get promoted'. The other part of the theory was that pay would decrease if you arrived late or you did not complete your timesheet properly. The belief was that by punishing you for bad behaviour, your performance would improve.

The science points out that this theory of motivation simply does not work. It shows that a third driver exists around human performance; the effective completion of a task is, in itself, motivating. Think about solving a puzzle. It simply is its own reward. Why do people paint, do crosswords or jigsaws? It's not because they are going to be rewarded or punished if they complete or don't complete the task. It's because they enjoy doing them. This is called intrinsic reward and has been proven since the late 1960s to be far more effective at motivating people at work than extrinsic reward, which is more commonly known as the 'carrot and stick' approach.

The problem with most business management thinking, even today, is that it has not caught up with the science of what motivates people at work. The majority of thinking about how to improve performance is outdated, not proven and is more rooted in myth than in science. However, business after business continues to put its faith in short-term incentive plans and pay for performance schemes in the face of all the evidence. They just don't work, and they hinder the development of a collective commitment-based culture. This type of 19th century thinking does real harm and it's more prevalent than less today. The science shows that organizations with clarity around purpose (we yearn to be part of something larger than ourselves), where values are used to create norms of behaviour and people are allowed direct control over their work and so have a strong culture, will be high-performing organizations on every financial metric. The core function of managers hasn't changed much in 100 years. Its central premise is control. Its main tool, the carrot and the stick. This is out of sync with our knowledge-based economy, where value is derived from ideas, innovation, relationships, insight and design, ie from people. The assumption underpinning this approach to people management is that without close oversight or the risk of punishment, people would happily do nothing.

It may seem obvious, but to create great business results we need leaders who understand how to develop, enhance and reinforce a culture that gets the most from the people who work there. Great leaders create purpose, direction and values to guide their people as well as processes to align and course correct, but they also allow their people to be as self-directed as possible. An inclusive culture allows space and a level of autonomy so that high-performing teams become the norm and the business is described as a great place to work by its people.

We need more leadership and a lot less management.

The often-quoted statement 'culture eats strategy for breakfast' is spot on. This means we require leaders who understand the importance of culture as part of developing a Competitive People Strategy. If you embark on a cultural transformation, the road will on occasions get bumpy because you are no longer just using a one-dimensional criterion of profit to measure success; you are seeking to balance values and profit against a central purpose when making key decisions. This commitment approach builds trust and generates huge amounts of additional discretionary effort from your people. Having a strong, inclusive, engaging culture delivers long-term superior performance.

It's also important to note that culture isn't static; it's always going to be challenged by people saying it's not as strong or as good as it once was, especially as you grow. A culture evolves over time but can be destroyed quickly. Leaders must protect the business purpose and values, the very essence of your culture, and thus avoid it being degraded. This will be an ongoing challenge. First, this will often be just nostalgia at play but people who were involved much earlier in the company's journey will be seeking a return to the halcyon days of the organization's step-up phase of early growth. However, it is a sign that you have a strong culture with a clear purpose and a dynamic set of values if your people are constantly paranoid that you are losing your culture. This signifies that they are passionate about it and believe it's important to the firms ongoing success. This is a good thing; it's important, it shows it matters. People recognize its importance and want to protect it.

CULTURE CHECKLIST

1   Review and reflect on the culture your business currently has. Does it need to change to enable improved, sustainable performance?

2   Does the business have a clear and robust purpose? Is everyone clear why the organization exists? If not, this is a great place to start.

3   Do you have a set of values that are derived from a process that included the extensive involvement of your people? Has everyone had the opportunity to participate in their creation? Have you involved other stakeholders, such as customers and suppliers, in the process?

4   How sticky are your values? Are they real? Can you provide examples of where the values have been used to make tough or difficult decisions? Have the purpose and values ever been used to overrule a profit or short-term business priority?

5   Do you have more leaders than managers? What is your organization doing to get the balance right?

6   Are you paranoid about losing your culture as you grow and develop? Does your leadership team spend time talking, thinking and exploring purpose and values on a regular basis?

References

Baron, J and Hannan, M (2002) Engage for success: Organizational blue prints for success in the high tech set ups, *California Management Review*, **4** (3)

Bock, L (2015) *Work Rules: Insights from inside Google that will transform how you live and lead*, John Murray

Coyle, D (2018) *The Culture Code: The secrets of highly successful groups*, Penguin

Gallup (nd) The Engaged Workplace www.gallup.com/services/190118/engaged-workplace.aspx

Hughes, D (2018) *The Barcelona Way: Unlocking the DNA of a winning culture*, Macmillan

Jones, JH (1994) *All Together Now*, William Heinemann

Pink, DH (2009) *Drive: The surprising truth about what motivates us*, Canongate

Sinek, S (2009a) How great leaders inspire action, TED Talk

Sinek, S (2009b) *Getting to Why: How great leaders inspire everyone to take action*, Penguin

Sorenson, S (2013) How employee engagement drives growth, *Gallup Business Journal*, June

Welch, J (2005) *Winning*, Harper Collins

06

Talent attraction

Why is talent important? Organizations have known for at least two decades that the attraction, retention and engagement of talented employees is strategically important. A survey by the Corporate Research Forum (2017) recently found that only 17 per cent of HRDs rated their organization as effective at predicting and planning for future talent needs, and only 20 per cent were satisfied at the outcomes of their business's talent management efforts.

As the world of work changes significantly over the next few years, talent will become even more critical to business success. Digitalization, automation and AI will combine with demographic forces to transform the nature of work, how it gets done and by whom. A McKinsey survey (2019) showed that 60 per cent of global executives expect up to 50 per cent of their organization's workforce will need retraining or replacing within the next 5 years. This level of enterprise transformation will require not just great leadership, but talent to reconfigure operating models, supply chains and the digitalization of services.

Another study, by PWC (2018), showed that 80 per cent of CEOs said that the level of skills and talent within their business was their number one area of concern, and additionally said it was a significant constraint on future growth. In a Mercer survey (Bravey, 2018) 80 per cent of organizations said that they feel their talent management programmes and practices need a complete overhaul.

Therefore, while all businesses recognize the importance of talent, most feel their current efforts are inadequate and that they are falling well short of their own expectations. My conclusion from all the data is that many businesses do not know how they should improve their systems to attract, recruit and retain talent.

What is talent?

In most organizations, when they consider what talent is, they refer immediately to technical talent and leadership talent. A great starting point when considering your talent strategy is to define what you mean by talent in the context of your organization, your foremost competency and how you intend to compete and win.

Let's start by exploring shortages in the labour market. While the media insists on using the term 'skill shortages', in fact there are three distinct sets of people shortages. First, we have labour shortage. These are entry level jobs where you can learn the tasks and acquire the skills in a few days. Think coffee shop barista. Within a week you can master the four areas of being a competent barista: (a) you can make great cup of coffee; (b) you can operate the till and take payment; (c) you can explain your product offering (the coffee, cakes, pastries and biscuits); and finally (d) you are nice to the customer. These four areas of competence can be learned quickly by almost anyone regardless of their previous experience. We have millions of jobs, often paid at the national living wage level or just above, that employers can't fill. This is happening in numerous sectors of the economy, including manufacturing, agriculture, retail and warehousing. This is a labour shortage, as the skill required to do the job can be taught quickly and easily.

Second, we have true skill shortages where we don't have enough skilled or experienced people to fill all the jobs available. In 2008, research carried out by the Recruitment and Employment Confederation highlighted there were three big areas of skill shortage: engineering, digital and IT. Ten years later we had close to 75 areas of skill deficiency. These included professional roles in HR, marketing, finance and sales but also doctors, teachers, electricians, chefs and HGV drivers, to name just a few. This brings me to talent. Skill and talent are different sides of the same coin. Skill is the core competency to do the job, talent is the ability to add more value to customers and make the organization even more successful. While I was at Royal Mail as HR Director of the Letters Business, we used these three descriptors of talent we wanted in addition to core job skill and experience:

1 The ability to think strategically but also roll up their sleeves and make things happen. This isn't 'ivory tower' strategic thinking; it's pragmatic 'make a difference' type ability.

2 Change orientated; they always sought continuous improvement and innovation and they could live with ambiguity and complexity.

3 Able to inspire and motivate others.

Finding people with skill is hard in today's job market; but finding talent is even more difficult. In a 2018 CBI survey, for example, 56 per cent of employers said they had difficulty filling all the jobs they had available.

The second factor here is that as talent becomes more important to commercial success, but is harder to hire and retain, then the employment relationship shifts from being employer driven to one where the talented individual who has the ability in demand can call the shots. Talent has a choice of where and how to ply their trade.

The changing environment for talent

One area where we have seen a significant shift in the last decade is who is accountable for a person's career. Whereas once this was believed to be an organizational responsibility, it is now a widely held view that individuals are responsible for the management of their own career. Also, career paths or routeways have become more complex and less clear cut; the delaying and hollowing-out of the jobs in the middle of our organizations is hindering traditional vertical career progression. Many academics theorize this change has led to a decrease in employee loyalty and employee engagement as the old lifetime employment model is no longer the norm. I am not convinced of that, but this change has certainly created a more open conversation on development and progression between talented indi-viduals and organizations. The way in which talented people choose to work has also changed, with self-employment, freelancing or becoming an entrepreneur competing against traditional permanent employment. Those with talent have more choice than ever before, not just about where they work but how they contract and the method they choose to provide their skills and services through.

The talent market has itself changed with the arrival of professional networking site LinkedIn and others such as Glassdoor or Indeed, lubricating the movement of talent from one role or employer to the next. This is likely to increase as talent platforms seek to move beyond just gig working into all forms of employment and contracting.

Social factors are also changing the jobs market around the world as older workers choose to remain employed beyond the traditional retirement age. By 2020, Millennials are set to form 50 per cent of the global workforce (KPMG, 2017) and we have yet to see what the impact of their different value sets will have on how they manage their careers. It is clear they have a more entrepreneurial mindset and they seem keen on starting a business or becoming self-employed at some point in their working life. However, as all these trends play out over the next few years, the only certainty is the growing importance of talent acquisition and retention.

How can organizations prepare for the talent crisis?

It seems clear that employers need a more expansive and dynamic view of talent supply and attraction; employers are starting to respond by moving away from traditional role descriptions and instead have become more focused on people's underlying skills and capabilities. Businesses will become better at defining the skills and abilities they require, while also recognizing the potential within their current work force. The planning element of a people strategy will come to the fore as organizations come to terms with talent and capability being critical to improved performance. They will want to ensure that they have defined their requirements and looked rigorously at the current work force, so they can develop the potential they already have while also defining what they need to go to the market to hire.

Talent strategy

In the next decade, organizations will seek to improve how they define their future talent requirements. Workforce planning doesn't happen effectively in the majority of organizations. Those that do undertake it often use a mechanistic form-filling process that leaders and managers don't value. This process will become an essential part of the delivery of the people and business strategy, so it needs to be reinvented.

Three planning phases are needed:

1 The business strategy and goals should be used to identify critical future capabilities (skills and talent) as well as highlighting critical roles in relation to organizational performance.

2 A dynamic workforce planning process will identify what organizational talent is needed to fulfil present and future demand. An external assessment and mapping process should also be undertaken that reviews demographics, projected skill/talent shortages and workforce trends in the markets the firm will be competing in or intending to operate within. This should also identify capacity requirements by location to enable effective macro and micro planning to take place.

3 A plan needs to be devised using a mixture of the following five talent strategies:

a. Build – reskill and upskill. Increase the hours that can be deployed from the current workforce who possesses the right capability. Define how staff will be developed so you can meet future requirements. The final area in building capability is to reshape jobs and projects to maximize their development potential.

b. Redeploy. One way of dealing with a surplus of skill in the short term would be to rent out your talent to other employers so that the company retains access to the expertise rather than letting people go and rehiring at a later date, which is a very costly process. Skills that will no longer be required in the same volume in the future should be identified and the opportunity to reskill people over time created.

c. Acquire. This will be a mix of approaches. It will include hiring new people now who have the right talent to meet your firm's future requirements. Another growing trend is to use fixed-term or temporary contracts and then hire from this population. The 'try before you buy' approach reduces hiring mistakes and provides cost-effective and flexible resources. An additional area that I suspect will grow is organizations acquiring whole businesses because of their business-critical capability. We have seen this in Silicon Valley where tech companies acquire early growth businesses, not for their product or intellectual property, but for their fundamental capability, ie their talent.

d. Release. This involves identifying skills that are not going to be in demand in a few years' time. This will enable the organization to use natural attrition and voluntary redundancy to right-size the business. This may also include the divestment of business units or divisions. This can all be undertaken in an orderly and thoughtful way if it is identified early. The plan can then minimize any painful redundancy programme.

e. Rent. This could take the form of strategic partnerships with other organizations. It could be an outsourcing opportunity where the delivery of activity is given wholesale to a third party. It could also involve the use of freelancers or contractors when the requirement is unlikely to be an ongoing, permanent requirement.

A coherent workforce plan should utilize a mixture of approaches including building, acquiring and renting capability. The plan should also provide clarity, not just on the competencies required, but should also define where and when it is required so the company has a comprehensive workforce plan.

Critical roles and performance

A key element of connecting business strategy with talent management is to identify business-critical roles – those that have the biggest impact on the organization's ability to build and sustain competitive advantage. This is often where companies should focus their talent investment. The identification of critical roles should also be used to ensure that your best talent is deployed in these jobs.

It is a commonly held belief that performance is normally distributed across the whole employee population. This idea was reinforced by forced distribution, which was used extensively by Jack Welch (while he was CEO at GE) and others during the 1980s and 1990s (Alsever, 2008). The assumption behind forced distribution was that that managers are often reluctant to differentiate between employees in reviews or appraisals. Forced distribution does have a place in helping firms tackle poor performance and can be used to help to reinforce the importance of having a robust and rigorous performance management system. A normal distribution is thought to be 10–20 per cent of employees performing at exemplary levels, 10 per cent under-performing and 70–80 per cent deemed to be average performers. The main assumption is that performance is normally distributed; most employees are average performers and only a small group are star performers and another small group are poor performers. Forced distribution was used to identify star performers and also to ensure poor performance was addressed with a view that this in turn would improve the organization's overall performance curve. It is not as widely used now, but the underlying assumption about performance undoubtedly being normally distributed across a business prevails.

Recent research challenges the idea of a normal distribution of performance. It is suggested that a key group (approximately 20 per cent) of employees deliver the majority of organizational performance (as much as 80 per cent) (Hamm, 2010). This reflects Pareto distribution and highlights that knowledge-based work is less constrained by the limitations of machinery, tools or capital that tend to hold back exceptional performance.

The number of top performers may be slightly higher than a normal distribution would suggest, but the big point is that your high performers contribute far more value than traditionally assumed. Talent is far more important to organizational performance than most leaders recognize. However, the identification of which talent drives performance needs much further analysis. An exercise that I have undertaken with many leadership teams emphasizes this point: 'A plane crashes which has the whole leadership cadre (300 people) on it. As the only survivor, you have to pick 10 people to bring back from the dead to restart the company.'

People do the task individually and then compare their list with those of their colleagues. What always amazes the audience is that, of the 10 names collectively agreed upon, nearly half would not be on the star performers or talent list. One reason for this is talent has become synonymous with leadership potential, whereas this exercise highlights who is really adding value. It also really starts to question what we mean by talent. If we can get to the heart of value or wealth creation by testing our assumptions, we may well challenge our definitions of talent is and what are business critical roles.

Talent process to talent mindset

One of the common criticisms of talent management is that it focuses too much on the process of identifying talent and not enough on making sure those identified as such have opportunities to grow, develop and progress. What seems to differentiate those that are great at attracting, engaging and retaining talent has nothing to do with the talent management process or HR's role. The organizations that get it right have a pervasive belief that performance and competitiveness are achieved with a great culture that encourages everyone to grow and develop. These businesses know that without enough talent they won't be able to outperform their competitors. This talent mindset, which recognizes that finding and nurturing talent is a critical role of leadership, is held not just by the CEO and top team but also up and down the whole management hierarchy. The talent mindset, as I like to call it, is a passionate belief that to achieve your business ambitions and aspirations you need great people. In short, more effective talent management is not about improving HR processes; it's about leaders having a talent mindset where they seek to attract, nurture, grow and retain talent as a key business activity.

Attracting talent: Employee Value Proposition

Every business has a customer proposition; what it is offering to potential customers? It normally involves a compelling reason why a customer should buy from them. However, few companies are as creative or thoughtful about people. Why should talent choose to work for you? As talent is a critical a battleground for competitive advantage, we think more focus and rigour should be focused on creating a winning Employee Value Proposition (EVP).

In the battle to attract talent, you need to position your business as one that takes talent management seriously. You seek to hire great people, provide exciting opportunities, great development and a dynamic but supportive culture. Research shows that managerial talent wants to work in an open, trusting and performance-orientated environment. Yes, your people want to be well rewarded, but you can't make a great Value Proposition with money alone.

An EVP is the holistic sum of everything people experience and receive while they are part of a company. This includes the intrinsic satisfaction of the work, the environment, leadership, colleagues, compensation and more. It's about how the company fulfils people's needs and provides great experiences. In Chapter 7 we talk about the need for ongoing measurement of the employee experience, so you can identify where this is and isn't working. A strong EVP that is perceived externally attracts great people like flowers attract bees. A strong EVP (or employee experience) excites people so they recommit daily to give their best and feel passionate about their work and their company. The Employee Value Proposition is more than a fancy job page on the company website, or values written on the walls of the office. It is what people experience in the company every day.

Getting an EVP wrong

At Royal Mail, during our transformation process, we knew we needed to hire more commercially minded talent, and this was crucial to our turnaround efforts. An Employee Value Proposition had been developed at great expense and with extensive external support. It described an aspirational view of how the organization wanted to be rather than how it really was. The proposition and the brief given to search agencies talked about development, great leaders, coaching and work–life balance. When we took this brand proposition to market we were losing £1.5 million per day (BBC News, 2005). We were in crisis and no one was getting development and work–life balance! It was so far from reality as to be laughable. This brand proposition created huge problems for the business. The talent we did hire was not prepared for the organizational reality and felt we had over-sold the culture and brand to them. They were right – we had. They were either very dissatisfied or they left, both of which made the business transformation that much harder. This was rectified when we created an Employee Value Proposition that described the talent we were looking for. We talked about the crisis. We were looking for self-starters who wanted to make a difference from day one. We then started to hire the right talent for the journey we were on. The lesson for all organizations is twofold: first, authentically describe the business as it is; and second, while you want to describe your ambition and aspiration, don't allow this to be over-sold or to get too far ahead of the reality. Under-promise and over-deliver is the way to go so that people get positive surprises during both the recruitment and the onboarding process.

EVP = brand

For me, the most effective EVPs are those that operate as brands. What I mean by this is they make you feel something. They do that because they have something they want to change. These companies feel human; the founders and leaders tell us how the world could be.

These companies have a reason to exist over and above making a profit. They have purpose. We talked about this earlier in Chapter 5 on culture. However, you can't pretend to have purpose and a strong employee brand if you haven't actually got one!

Employer brands are transparent

Before the internet and social media, potential employees had no way of checking out what it was really like to work somewhere. They applied for a job and, if lucky enough, got selected, they turned up on day one and hoped for the best. Today, candidates don't want to make mistakes and so they do their research. They don't just look at the business website; they read employee reviews on Glassdoor and Indeed. They look at the Facebook pages and LinkedIn profiles of leaders and staff and review their Twitter feeds. They acquire a really good understanding of the business culture and what it is like to work there . It's so transparent today – there is no hiding place. Don't pretend to be something you're not; always be authentic.

HOW TO DEVELOP A GREAT EMPLOYER BRAND: A SEVEN-STEP PROCESS

1   Build a business case for investment. Define the outcomes to be achieved. Define what the difference will be of having a strong employer brand. Win the debate with your leaders and stakeholders.

2   Understand your brand as it is today. Establish your current state by gathering data, information and insight on what its like to work in the business today from the people that currently work for you. Also, get an external perspective from potential candidates about their perception of your business. Surveys and focus groups will give you enough insight to decide what your brand is and how positively it's perceived. It's always worth remembering that your employer brand won't change the businesses culture; it's a mirror, not a catalyst.

3 Once you have a good idea of your current employer brand, strengths and weaknesses, pull all your insights together.

4 Once you have a clear idea of where you are and where you want to take your brand, identify your key audiences. Your key audiences are the talent or competency that, if you hired them, would make a significant impact on business performance. This segmentation process is very important as it helps you set the tone and get the messages right for the audience you want to target.

5 Now build your EVP – identify core themes, and seek to differentiate your brand from your competitors for the same talent. Define what needs to change or be modified and build a detailed change plan to support the new EVP. Your EVP should clearly articulate the proposed new deal – what, as an employer, you are seeking to provide for your talent, and what you want in return. Don't forget to test and validate the new EVP with your key stakeholders and your target audience both internally and externally before launching.

6 The last stage before launching your EVP is to create a set of messages and build them into a coherent communication strategy. This should use simple, direct language that resonates with your target audience, avoiding management speak and buzzwords. Think about all the channels you can use to involve and engage your hiring managers. They are your brand marketers. You could use video, infographics, blogs and new web pages.

7 Only once you have your managers on board will you be ready to launch. Don't forget to take a serious look at your recruitment process at the same time. There is no point in attracting the desired talent only for them to drop out of the process because your recruitment approach does not live up to your new messaging and brand.

Rethinking recruitment

We have addressed why and how you should develop an employer brand. Once you have started to attract the talent to your organization, you will need to define the critical talent or primary capability you want to hire. Having identified your target audience, ie the talent you are seeking to hire, it becomes much easier to develop specific campaigns.

First, be clear on your three or four target audiences; this could be digital marketing expertise, brand builders, software engineers or general managers, for example. Second, be proactive. Identify where your target audience reside, both online and offline, and seek to build an ongoing conversation or relationship with them. Provide them with great content, data, research and insight on the things they are interested in. Recognize sometimes you will be talking to talent for years before you or they are ready for them to apply for a job with you. Think of this as building awareness of your EVP just as marketers build product awareness amongst consumers before they decide to purchase. Third, make it easy for them to apply when the time is right. Ensure your candidate experience is effective and that you won't lose talent you have spent a lot of time and energy wooing.

Don't fish in the same pond

Attracting the talent you desire is a competitive process. One thing that businesses need to review is where are they seeking talent? It often pays off to search in parts of the labour market that your competitors are not searching in. As diversity and inclusion become ever more important issues for staff and stakeholders, leaders need to ensure they are attracting talent from as broad a population as possible. Groups that are currently under-represented could be ripe for targeting when looking for new talent. The language used in your job advertisements and on your online job site needs to be engaging and the messages tailored to the audience you are targeting. One example of thinking creatively about your audience is to consider those that want to work flexibly. A study for Timewise, the part-time job board, found that only 11 per cent of the jobs advertised in the United Kingdom mentioned flexible working (Steward, 2018). At present, well over 8.5 million UK people choose to work flexible or part-time. If you already work this way and enjoy it, you are excluded from 89 per cent of the jobs available! Women tend to work more flexibly than men, although that is changing. Therefore, without any thought, businesses are discouraging talented women from applying for their jobs because they have not thought to mention flexibility. More job seekers are looking for flexibility. In fact, it is climbing up the table of candidates' key preferences when they are looking for a new role. By just changing your job adverts, you could attract more high-quality talent. When developing an attraction campaign, identify pools of talent that are not presently applying for your roles. Do some research as to why and then develop a proactive approach in reaching out and encouraging them to apply; this is a great way to find and hire new talent.

Internal talent pipelines

Before embarking on searching for talent externally, make sure you have an internal talent management system, so you can search your internal capability before going external. With the online tools available today, it's so much easier to manage internal talent. In your HR system you should have a robust profile and data about all your people. This can be used to search and match internal candidates to the roles available. More than this, the data should enable you to forecast three to five years ahead. In this was you can build a talent pipeline so that you can test how strong your forward-looking talent pipeline for critical talent is. This should feed into your workforce plan and it will also help you focus on the development required to strengthen your internal pipeline. It will enable you to see gaps in your succession process, so you can plan external talent hires well before it becomes business critical.

The great news about growing your own talent is twofold: they know, and have been successful in, your culture; and you have been able to follow their development closely so the risk of appointing them is that much lower than for an external candidate. Great businesses with a strong culture and good employee experience normally get the benefit of growing a large percentage of their own talent. However, it needs an easy-to-use process and dedication.

The recruitment process: Make it a great candidate experience

If the candidate is the customer of the recruitment process, then their experience is critical. If your recruitment process is longwinded, complex and time-consuming and you get a high drop-out rate, you may well be missing out on talent. Once you have attracted both internal and external candidates into your recruitment process, the objective should be to make the process as easy and enjoyable as possible. I was astonished to learn from a REC research report called *The Candidate Strikes Back* (2015) that 80 per cent of candidates had never been asked for any feedback about their recruitment experience. If we want to create a great candidate experience that retains talented candidates in the process, then surely asking for candidate feedback at different points in the hiring process makes sense? This will enable you to learn what is working and what needs to be improved in your recruitment process. Candidates' expectations are not impossible to meet; all the data points to candidates wanting the same thing when applying for a role:

- Explain the process to me at the start – help manage my expectations.
- Keep me informed of progress throughout the process – no news is still news for a candidate.
- Give me the opportunity to show my best self – don't just use an interview to select.
- Make the process simple for me – make it easy to apply and ensure I get updates.
- If I've invested significant time and been through an interview or selection process, please provide me with constructive feedback even if I didn't get the job.

This seems to be a set of expectations that most organizations should be able to meet. It does require some thought and a degree of effective organization, but it feels achievable. However, candidates constantly say that applying for jobs is becoming more time-consuming, exacting and complicated. The candidate experience is getting worse, not better!

This provides you with the ability to differentiate your business from the rest. By reinventing your recruitment process you can become world class and create a competitive advantage at the same time. Your company needs to keep the process simple, use technology where possible, but also endeavour to keep the human touch where it's needed. Make promises you know you can keep and make the experience as personal for the candidate as possible. Be fair, be thoughtful and use candidate feedback and data to help your team improve your process.

When using recruitment or HR technology, be it a customer relations management (CRM) system, applicant tracking system (ATS) or HR system, let's make sure it makes us more effective as well as more efficient. Technology has been one of the reasons that the candidate experience has deteriorated over recent years. An over-reliance on technology in the hiring process can provide an awful experience in many situations. I recently attended an event where candidates were explaining how poor some employers' recruitment processes are. Two examples stood out: one where a candidate applied for a job with a big well-known UK retailer that they thought they were well qualified for. They were told that they had most of the required skills and that they should take an online test. This took them well over an hour and a half to complete. Once they had submitted the test, they received an automated reply saying they would hear in the next 48 hours if they would be invited for interview. After three days, they had heard nothing, so they contacted the employer online and asked for feedback. They still heard nothing. They tried again another two days later and yet again received no reply. The individual said not only would they never apply for another job with this firm, but they had also discouraged friends and family from applying. It gets worse; he was so disgusted with his experience that he and his family will no longer shop at this retailer. This poor recruitment experience has not only lost the retailer potentially good quality candidates, but it has lost a whole family's lifetime of shopping revenue.

Another similar story. A candidate had to fill in an online application form and complete an online test. They, too, were told that they would receive a response within three working days. They received a one-line email reply three weeks after completing the process saying:

'Dear Candidate, You have not been successful in your application.' This is marginally better than the previous person's experience in that they did get a reply. However, it didn't use their name and it was two and a half weeks late!

One way to constantly test your recruitment process and to review its effectiveness is to apply for your own roles. By playing the role of a candidate, you can see how effective and responsive your organization is at processing your application. It also seems like good practice to occasionally get a third-party organization to anonymously try out your hiring process from beginning to end.

While technology can make the hiring process more efficient, it may be making it less effective as great candidates are excluding themselves from your process. Talent has a choice; treat it badly and it will go elsewhere.

Selecting talent

We know that a curriculum vitae (CV) is just a snapshot of a candidate. It depicts a person's previous role(s), their education and qualifications and, if you are lucky, mentions their skills. Yet the majority of organizations still use the CV as their core initial screening tool. CVs don't provide any detail on a candidate's ability to do the role you have available. What employers need is an assessment of fit between skills and competency of the candidate and the role available. So online assessment tools have a place to help with the initial matching process. However, let's make these easy to complete and not overly time-consuming, otherwise the truly great candidates won't apply. As we saw in Chapter 4, interviews are a poor predictor of ultimate job performance. Line manager and one-to-one interviews are, however, still by far the most common selection process used.

It is worth paying attention to the features of effective selection from the organizations that get it consistently right. They recognize two fundamentals:

• Test and observe people while they are doing activity as close to the reality of the job as possible. So, if you are hiring a customer service person, you get the candidate to talk to real customers, or people role-playing your customers, in realistic situations, either face-to-face or over the telephone. This gives you a much better chance of assessing people's ability to undertake the role successfully. As part of the selection process, you can design an assessment centre to cover the majority of core job activities. This will give the candidate the best opportunity to show their skills, attitude, experience and ability relevant to the role's requirements.

- Get as many people from the organization as possible to view or observe the candidates during the selection process. The people used in the process can include team members, ie peers, other managers who will interface with the role holder, plus the hiring manager. This diversity enables different perspectives to be input on the merits of each candidate having undertaken the same exercise. This collaborative approach to hiring has been shown to reduce bias, especially unconscious bias. As importantly, it radically improves the likelihood of selecting the best candidate for the role.

Using a search firm

The search industry is being disrupted by employers seeking to do more of this activity themselves. Technology is making potential candidates more visible and contactable and there is also a growing shortage of candidates for senior roles. However, for leadership hires or critical roles, the use of a search firm still has considerable value. The art of finding, wooing and convincing talent to leave one good business to join another should not be underestimated. The craft of search consultancy seems to be even more important because talent has a choice about where it works, so convincing people to move role is a critical skill. The opportunity for small niche search firms to grow and compete against the traditional international search business has been enhanced by technology. Sam Allen of Sam Allen Associates explained that the search firm of the future needs to be able to work across borders, to be a cultural fit expert, possess the craft of wooing candidates, plus the ability to deal with the growing challenge of executive pay. If they can also add value by assessing and helping develop your top talent, they will then become even more important to organizations in the ongoing search for talent.

The cost of getting recruitment wrong

The data is very clear that we all get hiring decisions wrong. The key is to avoid making regular mistakes and making sure you avoid the obvious pitfalls. In a REC research report, *Perfect Match* (2017), over 85 per cent of HR leaders admitted they had made a hiring mistake in the last year. What is even more worrying, over 33 per cent of the same audience also said that they didn't believe that it had cost the business anything. This highlights one of the core issues with recruitment; leaders and managers don't understand the significant cost of poor hiring decisions. Recruitment is seen by many as a transitional, easy-to-do process or add-on to their core job rather than being something to be taken seriously. As a leader, hiring talent should be one of their most critical tasks and should be done professionally and effectively. The importance of getting the right people in the business is recognized but the critical significance of your employer brand, candidate experience and an effective selection process are still very much undervalued.

In exploring the cost of hiring mistakes, the REC report stated that employers recognized, when directly asked, that poor hires have a negative impact on staff morale, performance and productivity. They also recognized that the direct costs of advertising, training and any agency fees were often being repeated. They estimated the cost of getting a middle manager or professional (£42,000 salary) hire wrong was over £132,000. That's a ratio of over three times the salary cost. If you identify the number of poor hires in your organization in any one year (the average is believed to be about 20 per cent) and multiply that by three times their respective salaries, you will see that the cost of getting recruitment wrong is very costly. In a business that hires just 200 people per year, and by applying the 20 per cent failure rate and the average cost, the expense of getting recruitment wrong could exceed £5.2 million.

This of course also excludes all the great candidates that didn't apply, dropped out of the process or weren't selected. This opportunity cost is difficult to quantify, but even just using the transaction calculation above, you can see how important it is to ensure that talent attraction, selection and recruitment process is effective. This should be recognized as a critical, measured, reviewed, tested and invested business process.

Onboarding: The forgotten part of hiring

Onboarding is frequently overlooked. However, if onboarding is not undertaken effectively, it has the ability to undo all the great work completed through the talent attraction process, including providing a great candidate experience and selecting the right person for the job. A *Harvard Business Review* article (Bauer and Erdogen, 2017), suggests that companies lose 17 per cent of employees in the first six months. Most firms are competent at the administrative element of hiring. They send an offer letter, they tell the organization about the new person joining and will then often expect a line manager to pick up the whole onboarding process. Having spent a significant amount of time and effort finding the right person for the role, this seems at best inconsistent and potentially a very random way of organizing a critical element of the hiring process.

Again, even the term 'onboarding' brings to mind checklists and 'day one' activity, sorting out the new hire's technology, introducing them to people and showing them where to get lunch. We should not underestimate the impact of a friendly and welcoming first day or week. However, the real value is about getting people up to an acceptable level of performance in their role as quickly as possible. New joiners, when asked in research by the head hunter, Egon Zender, reported that almost 60 per cent took six months and another 20 per cent nine months to have full impact in their roles (Triantogiannis, 2017). The key seems to be helping new joiners understand the norms, culture and 'how things get done around here'. In fact, the number one issue cited by the 588 vice presidents or above interviewed by Egon Zender was their poor grasp of how the organization works.

One major opportunity often overlooked by businesses is to use the time between the formal offer and starting on day one to prepare the new hire for the role. This period is a great opportunity to bring forward the socialization process. A growing trend is to bring the new starter in to meet the team before their official start date, allow them to attend company events and an early appointment of a mentor (someone they can ask lots of questions of), to help them assimilate into the organization before they formally start.

A plan developed in association with a mentor and the line manager that starts with getting the basics right but goes on to focus on how the new hire is integrated into the organization and how they are supported in the first few months after joining seems critical. The mentor should be someone who has been in the organization for a while, often a peer, who can provide the informal information needed to get the new hire up to speed quickly. The mentor should have been developed so they have coaching skills and clarity about the role, its purpose and the business expectations of this task. The objective of any onboarding process is to get the new hire through their learning curve as effectively as possible, and a mentor facilitates this process. It's also good to have regular check-ins with new hires; we propose an informal conversation with HR after two weeks and again every month for six months. This is so that any signs that the hire is struggling to adapt or get up to speed is tackled at the time rather than allowing the whole process to fail.

TALENT HIRING CHECKLIST

1 Define what the term 'talent' means for your business. Have you identified critical roles?

2 Review your Talent Management Strategy and approach. Do you have a robust workforce plan that defines gaps and your proposed approach to address these gaps over time?

3 Think about performance in relation to critical roles and talent. Recognize that 20 per cent of your people produce 80 per cent of the

value. Have you defined the critical roles and what top talent looks like for your organization?

4 Do your leaders have a 'talent mindset'? Do they recognize that talent has a big impact on performance and productivity, and do they fully engage in regular reviews?

5 Have you got a robust Employee Value Proposition? If not, have you built the business case for the development of an employer brand to help you attract the talent you need?

6 Have you reviewed your recruitment process? Do you measure the candidate experience and use this to improve your recruitment activity?

7 Do you use tests and assessment centres to select people for senior or critical roles? Do you involve multiple people in the hiring process?

8 Have you reviewed the number of hiring mistakes your business made in the last year? Have you quantified the cost of getting recruitment wrong so that you can make the case for investment in getting it right more often?

9 Do you have a rigorous onboarding process for new hires using mentors to support line managers and an informal HR check-in processes to spot any assimilation problems early?

References

Alsever, J (2008) What is forced ranking? CBS News www.cbsnews.com/news/what-is-forced-ranking/

Bauer, TN and Erdogen, B (2017) On board them properly, *Harvard Business Review*, June

BBC News (2005) Royal Mail delivers record profit, 17 May http://news.bbc.co.uk/1/hi/business/4553933.stm

Bravey, K (2018) *People First: Mercer's 2018*, Mercer

CBI (2018) CBI Pentemps: Employment trends survey, August

Corporate Research Forum (2017) Rethinking talent management, CRF, November

Davies, B, Diemand-Yauman, C and Van Dam, N (2019) Competitive advantage with a human dimension: From life long learning to life long employability, *McKinsey Insights*, February

Hamm, T (2010) Applying the 80/20 rule to your employees', American Express www.americanexpress.com/en-us/business/trends-and-insights/articles/applying-the-8020-rule-to-your-employees-1/

KPMG (2017) *Meet the Millennials* https://home.kpmg/content/dam/kpmg/uk/pdf/2017/04/Meet-the-Millennials-Secured.pdf

Partner and Global Practice Lead (2018) Global talent trends study, May

PWC (2018) 22nd Annual CEO global survey, January

REC (2015) *The Candidate Strikes Back*, Recruitment and Employment Confederation

REC (2017) *Perfect Match: Making the right hire and the cost of getting it wrong*, Recruitment and Employment Confederation

Steward, E (2018) Timewise flexible jobs index, Timewise

Triantogiannis, L (2017) The first 90 days onboarding effectiveness to improve new executive integration, Egon Zender research

07

Employee experience

At the heart of a Competitive People Strategy is a core principle that you have to evaluate or measure the effectiveness of how your people are led and managed. It's the bridge between the business's purpose and strategy and what your people do at work every day. It also demonstrates both the effectiveness of specific people interventions. This chapter explores employee engagement and experience. It highlights its importance to cultural development and as a way of getting regular real-time feedback from your people about how good a place to work your organization is.

There has been a shift of organizational focus over the last five years from employee engagement to employee experience. Engagement is still the best way to measure how your employees feel about their job, work and the organization. Engagement is related to how effective an organization is at creating a positive attitude and behaviour amongst its employees. It measures the commitment level of your people and how this can be improved. If your employee engagement is positive, it has been shown to make an impact on organizational performance and productivity.

In Chapter 2 I talked a lot about how employee engagement can be used to gauge how effective the organization is at motivating, inspiring and communicating with its people and how it can play an important part in ensuring the business strategy is well executed. I also demonstrated the power of positive employee engagement in leading to improved performance and greater discretionary effort.

The way to think about employee experience is that it's a holistic view of your employees' perceptions about the organization, their work, environment and leadership that make a difference to employees during their time working in the business. Employee experience is a people-centric way of thinking about the business. It covers the whole employment relationship and, like a customer's experience, it changes over time.

By improving the employee's experience on a day-to-day basis, you will achieve increased engagement. Employee engagement can be viewed as the end goal, the outcome of a great or poor employee experience.

Employee experience (EX) covers so much more than a normal set of HR policies, procedures and ways of working. It's more than good onboarding, performance management and access to development. It involves the facilities (physical workspace), corporate communication and the tools (IT) to do the job.

The experience of the organization's leadership behaviour is also a key component of a good EX. Do the business leaders show integrity? Do they behave appropriately? Do they facilitate a workplace based on trust, openness and transparency? The employee experience aligns culture, behaviour and processes.

The employee experience journey

The employee experience covers the lifecycle of someone's employment and seeks to improve the experience at each stage of the journey from that of a candidate prior to joining the business, through onboarding, performance, development and, eventually, exit.

After someone has been employed for a few months, here are some of the aspects of EX you would be seeking feedback on:

- Does the colleague feel they have fair and equal access to development opportunities?

- During periods of stretch and when they are operating outside their comfort zone, is their physical and mental well-being supported?

FIGURE 7.1 The employee experience journey

- Do they have access to the technology and tools they need to do a great job every day?
- Do they get constructive feedback?
- Are they encouraged to learn and try new approaches at work?

Why are employee engagement and experience so important?

A 2011 study by PWC showed that employees most committed to their organizations put in 57 per cent more effort on the job and are 87 per cent less likely to leave than employees who consider themselves disengaged. A Gallup study (2017) demonstrated that companies with highly engaged workforces outperformed their peers by 147 per cent in earnings per share. However, the same Gallup research found that 87 per cent of employees are not fully engaged while at work. This is staggering data! Only 13 per cent of people at work are fully engaged. Therefore, only very few organizations are getting it right and potentially reaping the business benefits. This is a key component of a Competitive People Strategy; a differentiated employee experience leads to a more productive workforce, which over time leads to superior financial results. This demonstrates the business case for investment in people: people who are well treated, listened to and well led will deliver better results for the business.

How do employers provide a better employee experience?

A disciplined, insight-driven approach is needed to understand how employees currently perceive the organization, their leaders and their job. It's also important to get feedback about what they like and to identify the areas they feel should be improved.

Here are five areas to focus on when seeking to improve your employee experience:

1 **Treat employees like customers**

Marketers use customer experience (CX) as a key metric for a good reason. It tells them what a customer wants and helps them to introduce strategies that will attract and retain customers. It makes sense for leaders and HR to apply similar tactics to gauge the effectiveness of their employee experience; to look for positives, 'What is working?' and negatives, 'What do we need to improve?' We know that unengaged workers are unproductive, so focusing on engagement and what creates a good experience should be a business priority.

In a world where almost anything can be customized, employees are demanding tailored, personalized talent practices and consumer grade experiences while at work. Employees today behave much more like consumers than traditional employees. This highlights the importance of the employee experience; it needs to be of the same quality or higher than what your people receive as consumers. This establishes some benchmarks about how you treat your employees. As Richard Branson says, 'your people come first; treat them well and they will treat your customers well' (Branson, 2006).

2 **It's more than the money and the benefits**

People increasingly want more from work than just the pay cheque. They want flexibility, autonomy and learning opportunities. They are also concerned about how the organization behaves and the integrity of its leaders. Millennials, now the largest workforce generation, for example, value their voice being listened to, quality of life and status. The major difference with previous generations is the speed with which they expect their demands to be fulfilled. They shop around for jobs more than previous generations, using much wider criteria than just the salary and benefits package. Candidates are becoming more discerning and are interested in the business's values, culture, leadership and its role in society (corporate social responsibility).

3 The workforce will become liquid

Companies are becoming more like ecosystems and so need to think beyond their own four walls. In addition to permanent employees, workforces are now made up of people working in a range of different ways, including part-time, interims, freelancers and contractors. What is your non-employee experience like? Those that value flexibility and see themselves as being self-employed are becoming strategically more critical to business performance. Business after business seeks to keep fixed costs down while improving both the skill and talent available to them. Do you treat this critical talent well and do they feel valued?

With an increasingly large percentage of the workforce working in this way, this is not a side issue any longer. This flexible talent provides significant value, so how you treat and engage your non-employee workers will become a much bigger talent strategy issue going forward. Retention, productivity and performance maximization for this population will need to become part of a well-designed and executed employee experience strategy.

4 Technology is an enabler

Technology is playing a much larger role than ever before in how employees perceive their employer. They expect to have collaboration tools and be able to use their own hardware in the workplace. Technology enables greater use of analytics and insights, so organizations can tailor the employee offering. The ability to use data to pre-empt employee issues is becoming more commonplace. Predictive people analytics will become a key management tool over the next decade. The ability to look at data and trends to predict performance issues or the likelihood of someone leaving will become widely used. IBM's CEO, Ginni Rometty, has recently claimed that their AI can predict which employees will leave a job with 95 per cent accuracy (Rosenbaum, 2019). IBM HR, which was developed with Watson to predict employee flight risk, also prescribes actions for managers to engage employees. Also, end-to-end HR systems will enable better employee and manager self-serve and integrated people services to be offered to all employees in a user-friendly manner. In the same interview, IBM's CEO went on to say that HR can be vastly improved with the use of technology, while also becoming more cost effective. She said IBM had reduced its global HR function by 30 per cent while providing a better experience.

5 Transform HR so it is responsive

Once you have an HR/people system that can be used to get employee data and insights, the focus shifts to improving the moments that matter to an employee. This may be the onboarding process, performance management or access to online learning. The development of new people, products or services, should be designed using an agile methodology and be co-developed with employees; involving them in the process will improve the chances of effective implementation because of employee buy-in. The traditional 'HR knows best' or top-down approach to people product and service development is outdated and often alienates employees. The HR function, and particularly the shared service and business partners, need to ensure they have a customer focused mindset and set of behaviours. This will be how HR service delivery will be judged in the years ahead. The question becomes, 'Are we providing a great employee experience, rather than just the cost-to-serve metric, which seems to dominate the measurement of the people function at present?'

The employee experience challenge

As many enterprises are in a constant state of transformation or change because of market and digital disruption, we will need to continually redesign much of what our employees do while at work. Amid the business turbulence our people may often feel overwhelmed and disengaged. Despite many businesses' best efforts at improving the employee experience, real engagement – the outcome of a good experience – remains low. As companies seek to operationalize a good employee experience, they are running into barriers. Programmes and touchpoints within the employee experience, like recognition, communication, learning, compensation and performance management, are spread across disparate technology solutions and functional responsibilities. This makes it difficult for leaders and HR practitioners, but it also creates difficulties for the employee. If you imagine trying to provide a seamless consumer experience from different IT systems and with different people owing just part of the process, is there any wonder that the employee experience is often inconsistent and not well managed?

This change is happening at a time when the idea of work–life balance is giving way to the concept of work–life integration, especially as newer generations enter the workforce with differing expectations. For many, the employee experience now extends beyond the physical workplace and the 9–5 workday. This shift has significant implications for leaders as they grapple with how tools and programmes are designed and delivered. One of the issues is how to integrate different aspects of the employee experience with each other so employees receive a consistent and integrated experience. Designing interventions that work together with a common goal is a near impossibility for leaders and HR in many businesses to achieve. Given these circumstances, many firms are seeking new ways to integrate a variety of technologies so the employee has a seamless and consistent experience wherever they are in the employee lifecycle.

What we are starting to see is employers starting to manage the employee experience across the entire organization in a more holistic and systemic way. The keys to success include:

- Communicate to your people consistently and constantly your company's raison d' être, its purpose, why it exists. A strong statement on the organization's purpose and what it is seeking to change means that engaging your people is more likely to be successful.

- Ensure leaders are change and people centric. Leaders who show they care and are able to balance the quest for performance with a desire to look after their employees significantly improve the employee experience.

- Know your employees; communicate and listen to them. Having an open dialogue with employees about their needs and utilizing analytics to understand their perspective is powerful. This feedback loop is a core requirement of improving the employee experience.

- Treat the business as a laboratory, not a factory. Test and pilot new ways of working and operating. Seek to involve your people in improvement activity using either Lean or Agile methodology. Experiment and iterate with your employees. Create an environment of collaboration and creativity.

- Empower HR or the people function. Seek to upgrade and heighten the value of the HR/people function. Make sure you have the capability and capacity within the people function to ensure they are focused on improving performance while also creating a great employee experience at the same time.

We need regular data if we are going to improve performance

If you have ever listened to or read a book about an elite athlete, you will recognize the training, dedication and effort necessary to achieve their sporting success. You will also know that these athletes use constant data and feedback to monitor what shape they are in. This enables them to course-correct their training and preparation. They want data on their speed, strength and other metrics related to their performance readiness. They use this constant flow of data with their coach to review and amend their training programme, so they arrive for the big competitions in peak condition.

Now let's think about the data your leadership team uses to review the readiness of the organization to optimize its people performance. In most businesses, the leadership team has very little people data on which to base its decisions; they are running the business blind. They will have recent data, current performance and forecasts for all financial activity, but few have it in place for monitoring the human side of the business. By not having strategic data on how people are performing or feeling, leaders are running their organizations with only half a dashboard. This cannot be acceptable going forward. Any strategy must have regular data on progress; what is working, what isn't, and insight on what action is needed to either course correct or improve performance.

This is a huge commercial liability, but also an incredible opportunity for companies that want to achieve elite levels of performance; the ones that want to make the step change from good to great will be those that measure the employee experience regularly across the organization and, like an athletics coach, use this information to amend the activity.

Business performance is a day-to-day activity. However, leaders with little or no data on where their people are in terms of their readiness and preparation to perform will struggle to optimize performance. Organizations first started measuring employee satisfaction in the late 1980s and early 1990s. This led to the growth of employee engagement surveys over the last decade. The vast majority of this data is collected via an annual staff survey! This is like training to run in an Olympic final but only having one timed training session in the year prior to the big event itself. You would have no idea of what shape you were in and if you were likely to win or come last. This, however, is how we choose to run our organizations – without the intelligence (data) to make evidence-based decisions.

The variables are high if you collect data this infrequently

A number of trends are encouraging companies to seek more regular employee data. The first is that employee expectations are changing. They expect to be treated as an individual and to be listened to. They want to have a voice and be able to express their opinions and views. Second, the tempo and speed within most organizations today requires employees to adapt and change what they do on a regular basis. This constant change means employees need to be more aligned and connected than ever before. These changes have led to organizations seeking to fully engage their employees by providing a top-notch employee experience that includes two-way feedback and a chance to influence organizational decisions.

A study by AON (2018) found that only 11 per cent of employers are collecting employee feedback more than once a year, so 89 per cent of businesses have only one data point on which to reflect and think about the people who create 85 per cent of the firm's value. It would not be acceptable to measure cash flow or profit just once a year, so why is it deemed ok for people?

If we are seeking a competitive advantage via our people, then having regular data like an elite athlete seems obvious and essential. The good news is that an increasing number of organizations are seeking to collect more data from their employees and use it to make positive changes, but the change is just not happening fast enough.

It seems that continuous employee experience measurement is required to accurately assess and then manage the level of psychological investment employees are likely to put into their work. We also need to collect people data at a local level (function, division and team) so we can benchmark and use the data to learn from each other and to prioritize where action is necessary.

What to measure

Engagement is easy to capture; it normally revolves around three sets of questions:

1 What do people *say* about the organization? Do they have positive or negative perceptions?

2 Will they *stay* with the organization? This tests employee loyalty.

3 Are the people *striving* or giving their best efforts every day? This is measuring discretionary effort.

The shift proposed here is to move to a continuous EX measure, ie a process of gathering employee feedback more broadly across the employee lifecycle at much more frequent intervals.

This approach is the next generation of measuring employee perceptions. The surveys can be long or short and should often be undertaken at specific points in the employee lifecycle, ie day one, two months into the new job, after an internal promotion, every three months and even on exit. By combining rigorous data and survey science with the powerful technology now available, deeper insights can be achieved. These insights will give the business a much clearer picture about how employees feel about working in your business. This more granular data at greater frequency will allow management to respond quickly to changing trends and to implement new interventions to address issues identified in real time. The nature of the ongoing measurement allows for the interventions impact to be evaluated to see if they are working or not using the same data collection process. This enables changes to be evaluated quickly so that what is working can be continued on rollout to other parts of the business. It will also highlight what has made little or no impact so it can be stopped and another intervention made instead.

Continuous EX measurement will be different for each organization and may change as business objectives change. The key for continuous EX measurement is that it should collect different kinds of feedback across the employee lifecycle. It is not just measuring engagement; it is looking to collect feedback and views on specific experiences and incidents giving leaders much more data on which to act. The data should also be driven down to the lowest grouping possible, while maintaining anonymity, because you are likely to get very different results across departments, divisions, functions and even buildings.

The rise of the feedback culture

Modern consumer culture has made instant feedback easy and this is now perceived to be just a normal part of doing business. It doesn't matter if you are buying a new car, have just returned from a holiday or had a meal in a restaurant, we are asked to complete a review. Think about the online applications that we now use every day like Uber or Trip Advisor. They are constantly seeking our views and feedback, so improvements can be made. Uber is a good example; not only does the passenger rate the driver, but the driver also rates the passenger or customer. The opportunity to provide feedback has increased exponentially in our consumer-driven world. People who spend eight hours a day at work believe they should also be asked to provide feedback and express their views on their work experience, and be listened to. This highlights the limitations of the annual survey. Gartner (2018) recognized employee experience as one of the key building blocks of creating a digital workplace. Online tools are now available to enable regular employee feedback. Also, employees who can see they have influenced decisions in their workplace take more ownership and feel more engaged. This we know will lead to their contribution increasing, and better business results being achieved.

Leading the way

I recently met a young man, Daniel Hulme, who was speaking at the same conference as I was. The subject was AI and its human implications. It was his ideas and practice about how people data and insight could be used to run and improve his business that got me excited. Daniel's business is called Satalia. From its inception, the business embraced radical transparency and psychological safety through trust.

Satalia married its unique approach to people with technology and data in the search for a better working environment. The organization created a tool called 'Semantic' to help them achieve their ambition to reinvent how businesses are run by providing greater openness and transparency (Petrova, 2017). Semantic collects data from a wide range of systems and applications used by employees, including Slack, Calendars, GitHub to HR and project management tools. This is a pretty special tool, which not many other HR tech vendors have developed or delivered on. However, it's the culture and employees' attitudes to the use of the data that is refreshing – they don't think it is intrusive or creepy. Daniel was very clear; you have to have a culture of trust to be able to use people data in this way. One of the first uses of the tool was to organize a transparent pay review for all staff, including himself as CEO – how refreshing is that? They used lots of data, but the view on each other's work held the most weight. This weighting algorithm then fed into their pay review process, which worked like this:

1 Every employee's pay was made transparent.

2 Each person publicly requested the pay rise they thought they deserved.

3 The aggregated data about each person's contribution to various projects was presented.

4 With transparent data each person was then allowed to vote on other people's pay request, indicating whether they thought it should be approved at the proposed level, below that level or even above that level.

(JLA)

The Satalia weighting algorithm kicked in to balance how people rated each other to avoid gaming. One piece of feedback from employees was they thought the voting itself should have been made transparent as well! The process has taught the company a lot about itself. They found women didn't request as high a salary as their male colleagues. The process helped close its gender pay gap.

As an organization devoted to self-organization, non-hierarchical structure, employee happiness and data science, Satalia is leading the way by using AI and data to help the business be better at engaging, motivating and creating a great place to work. What's so enlightening about their approach is the recognition that its combination of data and a supportive trust-based culture, which will deliver a new approach to people management.

Creating a good work experience

According to a study by Mercer, thriving employees or top performers are three times more likely to work for an organization that enables quick decision making (81 per cent versus 26 per cent) and that provides the tools and resources for them to do their job effectively (82 per cent versus 30 per cent) (Mercer, 2019). Personalized and simplified development plans are also an important ask from employees – more than half (56 per cent) of employees want curated learning to help them evolve their skills and prepare for the future of work.

High-growth firms are twice as likely as moderate growth firms to provide a fully digital experience for employees. The data shows the value of regular feedback and what employees truly value. Give them a dynamic, fast-moving workplace, the tools to do the job and help them learn and grow and you will be creating a great employee experience. Not only will these contribute to better business results, but they will also help the company retain talent.

The expected results

In today's climate of uncertainty and constant change, employees crave stability. This always emerges towards the top of employee feedback and is a major reason why they remain with an employer. However, over 33 per cent of employees also think that AI and automation will replace their job in the near future (PWC, 2018). The way to help employees feel secure while responding to changing market trends is to invest in training and development while also fostering a culture where leaders are open, honest and regularly demonstrate they care. Getting regular feedback from employees will enable the organization to see how engaged their employees are, and to respond quickly when things go astray and results deteriorate. However, it is also important that data is viewed alongside current business activity and reality. Employees' views are influenced by current events such as a big customer loss or a pay freeze. The causal relationship or impact of negative events should not be an excuse, but neither should you overreact to your employee data deteriorating if there are mitigating circumstances. In fact, it reinforces the causal relationship.

The linkage between a great employee experience and improved productivity

Most organizations at either a macro or local level don't calculate the simplest measure of productivity (the annual revenue of the firm divided by the number of employees). Even fewer firms benchmark this data against their competitors. A focus on increasing worker productivity alongside employee experience data will help leaders identify what are the key motivators and retention factors for each group of employees. Managers will be able to play an active role in identifying what interventions are likely to have the best impact on productivity, eg is it improving the office layout, the technology available, manager feedback or access to online learning?

It's now or never

In this digital world with increasing transparency, employees expect a productive, engaging and enjoyable work experience. The good news for organizations is if you get this right, it helps improve productivity, customer experience and performance. As organizations shift to a networked, team- and project-based structure, the employee experience becomes both more important and more complex to deliver. In some businesses, people have multiple roles and multiple managers.

The challenge is that over the last decade workplace productivity has not significantly increased, and we have not found a way to unleash our people's creativity and energy, even with all the new technology, social media and collaboration tools available.

Companies need a new approach to harness the potential of their only appreciating asset – their people – one that builds on the foundation of culture, leadership and engagement. They should focus on employee experience. HR or people functions traditionally address issues such as learning, reward, culture and engagement as separate independent programmes delivered by different teams. They often operate in their own silos. This will no longer work. All these HR products and services as well as great leadership, a wonderful working environment and up-to-the-minute technology, need to be delivered as a holistic and integrated whole.

A well-designed employee experience means your people will not receive separate or random activities, but instead an integrated experience that positively impacts on their daily life at work. The ongoing collection of employee feedback increasingly leads to people demanding a good end-to-end recruitment-to-exit experience from their employer. They are the customers of your employee offering and they, like consumers, expect a user-friendly, well-designed and well-executed experience.

Many high-performing businesses have found ways to enrich the employee experience, often by using an agile approach so new interventions are co-created with their people and they are piloted before being rolled out only when they are proven to work. Others have used 'hackathons' to collect employee insight and ideas as well as using them to help in the design of new approaches. A hackathon is a sprint-like design event in which all those involved in a project or service come together to review, explore and ultimately design a better project or service by the end of the day. The concept was started in the software development industry. Sometimes there is a competition element to the events with a focus on winning and prizes.

The process often starts with a presentation about the subject matter. The participants suggest ideas and form into teams based on their interests and skills. The main work of the hackathon then begins. This can last anywhere between several hours to several days. Sometimes, people stay overnight. The atmosphere is informal and involves eating lots of pizza!

Towards the end of the hackathon, there are usually presentations in which groups discuss their results. To capture great ideas and work in progress, people often post videos and blogs about the results and share links on social media. The idea is to create an open space where great ideas are shared, but ultimately it leads to well-designed solutions.

Design thinking is another useful approach in which new concepts and products are developed by design teams. It's often described as cognitive, strategic and a practical set of processes aligned to better design products, machines and buildings. It is an accepted innovation methodology. Design thinking encompasses tools such as context analysis, problem identification and framing, ideation, solution generation, creative thinking and prototyping. The core features of design thinking have been used to explore both people and cultural issues within businesses. They again create an inclusive, collaborative and people-centric way of creating new solutions to today's organizational problems.

Both these open, collaborative approaches are used to get employees (the customers) to help design any proposed improvements. The use of design thinking has also been used extensively when seeking to improve workplace culture and productivity.

Let us not underestimate the ability of applications and the new tools available to play an active role in providing improved experiences for our people. They can be used to deliver value adding and services direct to employees' mobiles. This often simplifies the provision of data and information to frontline employees and managers, which in turn will help them to do their job more effectively.

The demand for talent within business and the desire to improve productivity and performance in a human way will drive an increasing focus on the employee experience over the next decade. This is becoming an increasingly important element of competing for and engaging your workforce. The employer brand, the external presentation of your employee experience, will be either enhanced or diminished by the stories that your people tell others, including candidates, about what it's like to work within the company. This is why a strong employee experience delivers the double whammy of both improved business results and acting as a competitive differentiator in the attraction and retention of great people.

EMPLOYEE EXPERIENCE CHECKLIST

1 Seek to get the leadership team to recognize the importance of both employee experience and engagement. Provide data on the linkage between EX and productivity and performance.

2 Seek to move from infrequent engagement surveys of your people to frequent surveys at different stages of the employee lifecycle that can be analysed by division, function, business unit and even by office. This will enable you to view trends and patterns across the business, but also identify areas of strength and areas for focus and improvement.

3   Use EX data as marketing use CX data to develop new products or people interventions that will positively impact on the experience for your people.

4   Ensure you align your EX data with business information, be that customer experience or service, metrics, productivity and performance. Develop a model that shows the positive impact of EX on these business results.

5   Use the five key areas of focus to collect EX data and make an assessment of how good your business is against each.

6   Explore the use of Agile methodology and design thinking in the development of new people-driven activity. Ensure your people co-create new interventions and they are not driven from the top down.

7   Review external employee data on Glassdoor or Indeed, so you can validate your internal EX data.

8   Make sure your employer brand or EVP is aligned to your EX data so that you are not describing to candidates an aspiration but rather the reality of how people experience working for you.

9   Think about Satalia's use of people data and explore how you could develop approaches that create transparency, openness and a culture that is fair and consistent.

References

AON (2018) Employee engagement rebounds to match all time high, Engagement Report

Branson, R (2006) *Screw It, Let's Do It: Lessons in life and business*, Random House

Gallup (2017) The engaged workplace, Gallup

Gartner (2018) Gartner's 8 building blocks www.gartner.com/en/conferences/emea/digital-workplace-uk/why-attend/gartner-insights/infographic-digital-workplace

JLA (nd) Daniel Hulme www.jla.co.uk/artist/daniel-hulme#.XLSbBEhKjIV

Mercer (2019) With more business disruption expected, making organizations 'future-fit' is top of mind, new study finds www.mercer.com/newsroom/with-more-business-disruption-expected-making-organizations-future-fit-is-top-of-mind-new-study-finds.html

Petrova, D (2017) Does AI represent me? Satalia https://blog.satalia.com/does-ai-represent-me-8c6255b3287b

PWC (2011) Millennials at work: Reshaping the workplace, PWC

PWC (2018) Will robots really steal our jobs? PWC

Rosenbaum, E (2019) IBM AI can predict with 95 per cent accuracy which workers are about to quit their jobs, CNBC News, 3 April www.cnbc.com/2019/04/03/ibm-ai-can-predict-with-95-percent-accuracy-which-employees-will-quit.html

Sabet, M (2018) How not to be creepy while using employee data in workforce management, *Data Driven Investor*, June

08

Change and transformation

Many organizations are currently in the process of responding to change as market after market is disrupted by technology, differing customer needs and new competitors. Wherever we look, traditional business structures are being reshaped or significantly modified. Once successful companies are finding that their 'sure fire' formula is no longer working. The world is moving beneath their feet as traditional markets, industries and sources of advantage disappear under the impact of AI, machine learning and algorithms. As a result, the majority of business leaders now find themselves and their firms in need of reinvention. In response to these changes, organizations are becoming flatter, leaner, decentralized, and more agile and responsive.

Most corporate transformations have a poor success rate, despite the wide availability of advice both in the media and from self-proclaimed experts on how to undertake organizational transformation, and the fact that consultants and academics have significantly improved their understanding about how transformations should be led. It is accepted that about 75 per cent of change projects are unsuccessful, through either not delivering the intended benefits or through being abandoned entirely (Anand and Barsoux, 2017).

Three reasons for transformational failure

There seems to be three major reasons for this widespread failure.

The first is the wrong quest or goal is established at the beginning of the process. Often, businesses pursue the wrong changes, especially in the complex and fast-moving environments where decisions about what to transform in order to remain competitive can be taken hastily, often in a maelstrom of conflicting data. The pressure on leadership teams especially in listed businesses is immense. Analysts often require quick responses to changing market dynamics. Before considering the process of change, leadership teams need to work out what to change instead. If companies don't choose their transformation battle wisely their efforts will a have negative effect on business performance.

So how do leaders decide which changes to prioritize? They should ensure that they understand three things:

- The catalyst for transformation – what is causing us to do things differently?
- What is our core quest? Define the difference that would be delivered if the quest were achieved.
- Define the leadership capabilities required to see the transformation through.

The goal of any corporate transformation should be the creation of additional customer value. This would ideally consist of both improved efficiency (through streamlining, agile working and cost cutting) and reinvestment in growth. In my experience, too many change programmes fail because they focus far too narrowly and seek to make the organization leaner without seeking new opportunities to grow. Too many businesses become great at 'shrinking' but don't find ways of providing more value to customers. In many contracting or commoditized markets, firms get stuck in turnaround mode, chasing ever-greater efficiencies. Cost cutting or right-sizing projects can have merit but if they become an ongoing and constant focus then the cost reduction and restructuring will have a negative impact on innovation, creativity and morale.

The second area where firms get transformation wrong is in the choice of target. It's not uncommon for a business to have three or four defined objectives for their transformation. If a transformation has too many targets, such as innovation, customer focus, agility and going global, any transformation programme will be seeking to change too much at the same time. Each of the above transformational targets requires its own focus and enablers. It will often require a new operating model, new channels to market, changed processes and new ways of working.

The third area where mistakes are often made is the overwhelming priority given to structural change in many large-scale transformation projects. Two types of reorganization are often explained as important transformation objectives in themselves.

The first of these is restructuring. This consists of modifying the structural archetype around which the organization's resources and activities are organized, which typically includes function, business or product-line, customer segment, technology platform, geographic area or a combination of the above.

A second type of reorganization is called reconfiguration. This involves adding, splitting, transferring, combining or dissolving business units without changing the company's underlying structure. Often the rationale from leaders is similar; we seek to become more innovative and improve our financial performance. To do this, we need to reshape the business.

I am a great believer in organizations seeking to shake themselves up to reduce complacency and inertia, to remove ineffective routines and to remove management fiefdoms that slow growth. My concern is that a structural response to changing market dynamics alone will never deliver additional customer value. In an era of industry transformation with competitive advantage lasting ever-shorter periods of time, the leadership's ability to define and execute organizational transformation becomes an essential capability in itself. We need to change how we transform big companies. They often end up as bureaucracies, which saps their creativity and willingness to take risks that ultimately hinders productivity. As organizations grow they create clear lines of authority, specialized units and standardized tasks, and they use bureaucracy to help them manage scale. They use these ways of working to deal with the complexity that growth causes. This perspective that it is structure that is hindering progress often leads to transformations being driven from a structural perspective alone.

Royal Mail: From losing £1.5 million a day to £400 million profit

The UK's postal operator had got itself into a tough place in 2003. As we have already seen in previous chapters, it was losing over £1.5million a day – yes, a day! (BBC News, 2005). Its customer quality record was failing, its industrial relations were so poor that it accounted for well over 60 per cent of all the days lost to industrial action, absence was high, there was no new technology and what there was just didn't work. It was a once-great institution (Royal Mail had helped set up most global postal operations) and one that had remained profitable for most of its 400-year life.

The challenge for Alan Leighton (Chairman) and Adam Crozier (CEO) was to transform this organization so it was fit enough to thrive in a newly created, deregulated market. The regulator, Postcomm, was opening up the market to competitors for the first time and if you can't make money as a state monopoly then being up against young, hungry entrepreneurial businesses was not going to be easy or comfortable. I joined Royal Mail in 2003, first as the Chief Learning Officer (Change, OD and Learning) and then as the Human Resource Director for the 'letters' business.

We all knew that this transformation programme needed to operate at multiple levels at the same time. We needed to empower frontline managers to lead their people and create change, from the bottom up. We needed to provide our people with the tools for the job, including walk sequences and sorting machines. We wanted to reduce the power and bureaucracy of the centre, who were a dead weight on change. When I arrived the HR function alone was huge; we stopped counting the people in it at 4,000. We had a budget of £157 million just for HR. We knew that we needed to change things at a pace, and HR was where we needed to start by putting our own house in order. We were in crisis and so the change programme needed to operate in a counter-cultural manner. We decided we needed to break things before we sought to fix them. Even now, I get a cold sweat when I think about how we went about the early stages of the transformation. It was direct and, at times, brutal. This is an important learning point for the people leading the change. Every change programme is different; it's always context-specific, so what will work in one organization will often not work in another. Each transformation needs to be designed to meet its own specific requirements and recognizing the organizations culture, leadership, pressure for change and its mobility.

Transformation is context-specific

The learning for me and many of my colleagues was: we needed to start the change and make sure it was visible, dynamic and showed that we were serious. The organization had been trying to transform itself in an incremental way for over a decade with little success. If we had had longer and weren't in such a poor operational and financial situation we would have taken more time to analyse and been more careful and considerate, but in a crisis, you have neither the time or money.

For example, we restructured the HR function from top to bottom in six months, creating a Shared Service, Centres of Excellence and HR Business Partners. We removed hundreds of personnel people who were doing line managers' jobs for them. Our managers needed to manage their people and performance themselves, rather than delegating the difficult people conversations to their HR colleagues. This was also about HR sending a message to the rest of the businesses; 'We're doing this to ourselves first before we help you do the same!'

Hard and soft change at the same time

The objective for Royal Mail was simple: to survive. At one point the business was technically insolvent so survival was clearly the first objective. After that, we knew we needed to compete and thrive in a deregulated market place that was fast emerging.

We needed to show to our people that how we currently operated would not be good enough in this changed world, and while the change was difficult, we stated clearly that we wanted to take our people with us on the journey of transformation.

This led us to work on soft and hard change at the same time. A great example of this was improving on our absence record. We had, on average, over 12 days' absence per worker per year. This cost

Royal Mail £50 million in total for each day of absence. We reviewed our processes and could see we needed to tighten them up and ensure our managers were proactively managing absence. They needed to ask staff for doctors' notes, and we implemented a return-to-work interview. Repeat absentees were referred to Occupational Health. The unions were very unhappy as they thought managers were becoming over-zealous. This process of hard change included the design of new processes and policies. We trained the managers and modified reporting so that leaders could track performance at a regional level. However, this hard change was supported by some well-designed soft change. We created a competition for all posties who had not taken a day off sick in six months. They would be entered into a draw for a new car. In fact, we ran this in all 31 regional areas and across all central functions. In total we ran 39 competitions. The Chairman went around the country handing out new cars to 39 staff. The heading for the competition was 'You've Got to Be In It To Win It'. It created a huge buzz and showed that, as an organization, if we got better we were prepared to share the benefits of success with our people. We repeated the exercise at least three more times with different prizes each time, and by 2007 absence was down to six days per worker per year. This amounted to a saving of £300 million, while hundreds of staff benefited from new cars and Caribbean cruises. So, when designing any transformation process, always seek to find ways to link your people into the success of the change. You have to be able to answer: 'What's in it for me?' This doesn't need to be as explicit as my Royal Mail example, but you do need your line managers to be able to answer the 'why?' and 'what's in it for us?' questions.

Winning hearts and minds is never easy, but it is an essential part of any change programme. The psychological benefit of describing what the change will mean to your people is a very powerful change lever that needs to be utilized not just at the start of a transformation process but throughout its life.

Another personal example of transformation; I had just arrived as the new CEO of the Recruitment and Employment Confederation (REC) in 2008 when the financial crisis struck. Our industry shrunk by 30 per cent or £7billion in an 18-month period. Our members, while most retained REC membership, cut their training, qualification and research budgets drastically. They were seeking to survive the worst recession in living memory. This had a huge negative impact on our revenue and profitability. It meant we needed to transform the organization not just to survive the economic slow-down, but to be more effectively positioned for growth once we had survived the downturn. The first objective was to create clarity on our purpose; a picture of why we existed and why what we did was important – why the organization mattered. We were also brutally honest with our people that while times were hard, our future would be secure, and we would be well positioned for success and growth if we modernized and repositioned ourselves. During the process of change our people metrics all improved, team work got better than ever, managers coached, and I spent much of my time communicating with staff in small groups. The next year, 2010, we broke even and then the following year the returns on the transformation started to emerge. We made a significant profit; we acquired new members and we retained more members than ever before. They liked the new REC and what we had become. We provided more value and service while also having fewer staff who were nevertheless more capable.

As we started the process, people needed to hear the truth about why we needed to change. They wanted to understand the journey and they needed to believe that if we did what we said, the REC and they would have a bright future ahead. Honesty on the need for change, a clear description of what the change is and the impact it will have on the future of the business should always be communicated early in any transformation programmes.

Don't forget to explain what remains the same

Is it any surprise that people often don't buy into change or transformation? One major reason I have observed is that the change is over-sold. Leaders often get obsessed with talking to their people about the change, while not talking about what remains the same.

In the Royal Mail transformation, we changed the 104,000 front-line posties' jobs. We changed the times our people started work, we asked them to drive rather than walk or cycle, and we wanted them to use hand-held computers for the first time. These were significant job changes. We communicated what needed to change and why, right at the start of the change process. However, we didn't communicate what would remain the same for our people; they would retain their current walk, they would work at the same office, be part of the same team, wear the same uniform and have the same terms and conditions. By over-engaging and repeating the change message without balancing it, we created more uncertainty and fear than was necessary. We forgot to emphasize what would remain the same for our people. Once we recognized this and we started to balance the change messages and talk about the factors that would remain the same, we found it got easier to engage our people about how and when we should make the change.

This is a critical learning point for those leading change or transformation programmes. Seek to position what's going to change with what will remain the same. This balancing of the message enables people to accept the change as they can put it in context.

The metaphor for change

Most businesses have become preoccupied with the idea of finding ways to fix and control the work environment. We are always seeking to get more organized, so we restructure and reconfigure the organization so it is fit for purpose. The typical organizational diagram has neat and tidy boxes and lines. Historically, this mechanistic view of change worked, but I've been in business for four decades and can count on one hand the number of successful corporate transformations that have been focused on process and structure alone.

To unlock change in organizations we should start by looking at how we describe the business we work within. The language used to describe firms has not changed much over the last 200 years. We have a tendency to use mechanistic or industrial metaphors. We've sought to understand organizations as being equivalent to human machines and we have sought to design them and run them using this mindset. Hence, complex tasks and activities are broken down into their separate parts, given to different functions and then broken down again into separate jobs. The work is controlled through job descriptions, hierarchy and all sorts of sophisticated tools and reporting frameworks. However, it's only recently that people have started to recognize that organizations are not machines. They are made up of living groups of people who, in my experience, often refuse to act like cogs in a machine.

What is hiding inside each of our businesses is a set of assumptions that we rarely notice or consider. The culmination of these assumptions and practices is like an operating system that is silently running in the background. To understand this mechanistic mindset, you need to dig deep into an organization's assumptions, which underpin it. These include:

- People cannot be trusted to manage their own work without direction. They need to be told what to do.
- Work needs to be managed with an elaborate set of rules, policies and procedures so complex activity will be consistently delivered.
- We need to plan everything in detail and ensure compliance to the system with people checking adherence.

However, if you view the business as a human enterprise, you have a set of assumptions that will enable change to happen more effectively:

- People can be trusted to work together to do the right thing for the organization and its customers. They use their own judgement.
- Complex issues can be solved by people sharing, listening and talking to one another. Teams can find ways to best organize themselves and ensure the work is delivered to specification and to customers' expectations.
- We can monitor, review and improve our own performance. We don't need compliance and people checking up on every activity undertaken.

In summary, we need to start accepting that businesses are complex adaptive systems, not complicated mechanical ones. They are living systems, not machines.

Purpose, meaning and culture

One of the recurring themes of this book is that performance is improved when we create a purpose-driven organization, where people come together to achieve something bigger than themselves. Something that they feel is important and that will make a difference. This creates work with meaning. According to Gallup, only 13 per cent of people are engaged at work. People have needs, interests and inclinations of their own, and in my experience they rarely submit to the requirements imposed on them by organizations unless they are connected and engaged in the work and purpose of the business.

When leading transformation and change, we must find creative ways of organizing work that allow us to enable our 'people to work with the flow'. My favourite way of describing organizations is as cultures, or political systems. If we use the culture metaphor, we begin to understand how the organization is held together through patterns of shared meaning, shared values, ideologies, rituals and belief systems. If we view organizations as political systems, you start to look at conflicting interests and power plays, which clearly shape how work gets prioritized.

Designing transformation programmes

As machine thinking is so prevalent in Western businesses, when we come to think about change, we rarely grasp the full nature of the change required because we are looking at the organization through a one-dimensional lens.

Think about how organization charts and diagrams tend to dominate our thinking about organizational design. We, on occasions, may map the workflow but in reality, when talking about change, we too often start with structure. We turn it upside down if we feel that we are getting too hierarchical or remote from the customer. We de-layer and cut out the middle to streamline decision making. We downsize, re-engineer and divest parts to reduce costs and to improve focus. We move to matrix structures when we want to balance project working or align business lines and geographical operations. We talk about teams and team-based working when we know we need to improve participation.

Most structural change involves redrawing the organizational chart or reshaping the hierarchy. My favourite, by some distance, is replacing the solid lines with dotted lines... and so on!

If you start with structure in your transformation process, you often don't change the core issue; the basic problems remain unchanged. For example, if you downsize or reconfigure the organization, you usually just end up with a smaller bureaucracy! When you move to a matrix structure, you often end up with increased complexity or confusion. The most important point is that the change process will deliver many fewer benefits than if you changed in a more integrated and people-focused way.

Change to transformation

Transformation is different from large-scale change projects such as re-engineering or agile development. There are five characteristics that are always present in transformation:

1 Transformation is comprehensive in that it involves the whole organization and requires an integrated set of solutions. Transformation is pervasive, affecting structure, processes, systems, people, product/service portfolio, collective knowledge and skill as well as the organizations' environment (markets, stakeholders and regulators). Transformation requires more than 'single point solutions' that are chiefly incremental in nature. They may create change, but they won't produce radical shifts in business strategy and performance. The focus is to change the way the organization

performs or competes. Therefore, transformation is an integrated set of disciplines, approaches and interventions, united and configured so that far-reaching and substantive change is achieved.

2 Transformation often involves challenging some deeply held assumptions, including the fundamental purpose of the organization – what it does for whom and why.

3 Transformation often means radical performance improvement, not a 5 per cent improvement in operating profit. At Royal Mail it involved a £1.5billion turnaround in four years. At the REC we had to change every customer-focused process.

4 Off-the-shelf fixes do not produce transformation. Importing solutions wholesale from one business to another will simply not deliver deep-seated change in human behaviour. Consultant-led transformation programmes often fail because the analysis, understanding and deep insight developed in one organization is unlikely to land, be owned and to connect in the second or third organization on the conveyor belt.

5 Finally, transformation is far reaching; it leads to a dramatic change within the organization. Transformation needs to be recognized as an unnatural act; it shouldn't happen too often in an organization's life. At Royal Mail it took us close to 400 years before having to reinvent how we operated!

The four pillars of transformation

Waking up the organization

Leadership is about always about choice and making decisions. If you don't make choices, you're just an administrator. The first role of leadership in transformation is to wake people up to the fact that change is needed; not small-scale incremental change, but large-scale transformation. The leadership team need to start the process by holding up the mirror to the business and by describing the catalyst for change. They also need to create discomfort and unleash some of the inherent conflict.

When an organization is in need of transformation, an early human emotion is to find someone else to blame; who wasn't doing their job? My experience shows that taking people (the top three layers of leadership) through the process of discovery (where we are and why we need to change) is a great starting place. You should share the data, evidence and insight about why the organization needs to change. This shouldn't be rushed; it should involve a few weeks of collective work. The purpose is to enable people to see the scale of the challenge for themselves and to recognize that we have a choice; transform or die. The process of review should look at the business and organization through as many different lenses/perspectives as possible. The data collection process should involve suppliers, customers and other stakeholders. The outside world's perspective is always full of value and insight. People should be involved. An internal view of why the organization should change and how it can best serve its customers can also create a powerful narrative of 'why change'. The process will flush out ideas about the breadth of the change required. Also, it is important to review previous change programmes as this provides learning about how we are going to do it differently this time.

Ideas and vision

Having sought feedback and involved people in understanding the need for transformation, the business now needs to explore *what* needs to change. The leadership cadre leading the process must anchor the transformation in a core idea; this should focus on strategy, customer and growth or a mixture of all three. However, it needs to be expressed as one idea, so it is easily understood by your people. It needs to define the change required and explain the difference the change will make to customers, results and profit.

A defined goal or vision should be articulated, refined and tested multiple times. It must be deconstructed, ripped apart and tested so that it is owned by the whole leadership cadre. At this stage you can't have people still questioning the need to change and the broad thrust of the transformation. As the CEO of the Recruitment and Employment Confederation we used the phrase 'From good to great' to describe the journey we were on. We described our product/service offering, our website, our customer experience, the capability and all manner of things as good, but then described what great would look like and the benefits of achieving greatness in terms of membership growth, increased revenue and improved profitability. As a not-for-profit organization we also went further and described the virtuous circle – once we were great, we would be able to invest in our people, products and services. Before we started to change anything, the whole organization had a clear sense of the vision of the transformation. There was no doubt we needed to change; as we went through the initial processes you could feel the energy rise and momentum build even though half of the people in the organization would have their job changed.

During the early phases of a transformation process (the waking up of the organization and the idea collection and visioning phase), participation, conversation, debate and, to some extent, conflict are all good things. Emotional buy-in can only be delivered once you have given people the opportunity to participate, give their views, be able to challenge, question and help define the change process. They need to feel part of the process. Large-scale transformations that work are not 'top down'. You will know when this has been achieved because people will own and drive the change in behaviour themselves. They won't need to be told what to do and how to do it.

Building support

In my experience of designing an organization's transformation, learning, development and growth have always been central to the journey. If you want people to act or behave differently you need to support them through the process.

At Royal Mail this was focused on frontline managers; those that ran our delivery offices and the shift managers in our big mail centres. Historically, these frontline managers were challenged by the trade union, which was better informed and also had the power to influence which jobs people took, the leave they had etc. We needed our managers to take back responsibility for people. What became apparent very quickly was that the size of the change for many of our managers was huge. They didn't have the skills, confidence or the tools to do what we now expected of them in the transformation, so we made a huge investment in providing them with the information, tools and the skills needed. This involved direct face-to-face meetings with the Chairman and CEO every quarter. This took three full days every three months, with five sessions a day, to directly engage with all our managers.

These sessions were one-part communication, so frontline managers heard the leaders' views first hand, but, more importantly, they were collective therapy where managers could ask for help and describe the reality they faced on the ground, and the Chairman and CEO would seek ways to help in real time by removing barriers and blockages. We produced learning maps for managers, so they could brief their people every week at listening and learning sessions. We gave them training on giving feedback, making presentations and having difficult conversations. In a business where it was very difficult to change both what and how we did things, our managers' capability was critical. If we hadn't helped the managers grow, nothing would have changed. The greatest success of our leaders was to convince our people that they had to do things differently if the organization was to survive and thrive. The Operations Director, Tom Melvin, a Royal Mail veteran of 39 years, led from the front and spent a lot of time talking to managers across the UK on a day-to-day basis. He had an operational team who were desperate to make the change happen; who recognized this was a once-in-a-lifetime opportunity to save a business that they all loved. This led to real personal contact with managers and staff. The conversations changed, and frontline managers started to demand support and help. The talk changed as they described how they were going to change things on the ground. We were now mobilized for action.

Implementing the change

At Royal Mail we had to be brave and take tough decisions. Many of the leaders couldn't operate in the new environment we were creating.

We treated people with respect, but some were clearly not going to make it and we had to make tough calls because we needed to build energy and momentum. The Head Office, which had been the traditional 'top down' hierarchy, was reimagined as the Support Centre to the operation. We empowered frontline managers to make change happen on the ground. Perhaps the best example of this was the removal of the second daily delivery service. We used to visit every house in the United Kingdom (28 million addresses) twice a day. The second delivery represented 20 per cent of the cost base but we only delivered 4 per cent of the daily post. This had been known for many years and we had Change Team at the centre working on this. This team had an MD and over 350 people working on it. They had modelled every postman's walk around the country and were always going out to test the model with the local managers and posties. What became clear was that the posties and the managers in the delivery offices thought the team from the Centre were fair game, so they would provide a whole set of changes; new estates, doing the walk in a different order. The team from the Centre would note all the changes before going back to the Centre. This process had gone on for years. The Centre believed they knew best and were the right people to design the change process. They believed the operators weren't clever enough to design the walks to remove the second delivery. In fact, one of the best decisions we made was to abandon the Central Team and their model. We gave the Delivery Centre Managers and their teams the task of designing the new walks in their office. They had three months to do it and make the 20 per cent saving. We gave them the tools and development, but it was their choice. The change was made to time and the budget savings were delivered. Operationally, our quality figures went haywire for a few weeks, but they settled down within the month. This demonstrated that if we trusted our managers and their frontline staff to lead the change, we could do big things quickly. It built confidence and was a positive way of reinforcing one of our transformational messages: that we all had to change, it wasn't going to be imposed from the top or the centre, it was going to be undertaken in a collaborative and participative way.

Leading change

The role of the people or HR function in transformation and change is that of leadership. The people strategist or architect that we propose in Chapter 10 should be one of the organization's major transformation designers and implementers. The lead people person and their team in future should have the capability, skill and experience to lead the change process. They should have the diagnostic tools and experience to design an iterative, participative transformational process. The people strategist or architect is the right person to help the CEO lead the transformation because people change is always the hardest part of the process and it's also the most important element. The mindset and behaviour changes are often the drivers of the whole transformation, not because people are given data or analysis but because they are shown a truth. This positively influences their emotions. This is especially true in large-scale organizational change, where you are dealing with the introduction of new technologies, new ways of working, cultural change, globalization and the core business strategy.

In this age of abundance and turbulence, where people want to be recognized and listened to as individuals, if you handle people or the emotional side of change well, you have a head start. If you handle the people side of change poorly, it will drive you crazy, cost a great deal and cause even more pain!

The process described above has people at its centre. The central challenge is not strategy or systems, or even culture. These elements and many others are important, but the core issue, without question, is behaviour – what people do, and the need for significant shifts in what people do, on a day-to-day basis. The heart of any organizational transformation is working with your people's emotions. The flow of see–feel–change is the most powerful way to lead on organizational transformation processes.

The change will never stop

Turbulence will never cease. In fact, most evidence suggests that businesses will need to change, refresh and realign more regularly in the next decade as a new wave of technology including AI, machine learning, IoT, algorithms and 3D printing create new ways of working and automate up to 38 per cent of the jobs in the UK and around the world (PWC, 2018). The issue is that participatory change is powerful; in Chapter 7 we mentioned hackathons and design thinking. These types of processes are energizing, cathartic and creative. The challenge is, how do we execute business as usual while also learning and changing at the same time?

The rate of change is not going to slow down anytime soon. Enterprises everywhere will be presented with huge competitive challenges and potentially wonderful opportunities at the same time. Very few businesses have been effective at adapting to a fast-changing environment over the last two decades. Structure, systems, practices and culture have often been more of a drag on change than a facilitator. As environmental volatility continues to increase, as most predict, organizations' core competency will become the ability to adapt at speed. The whole enterprise needs to be more agile, responsive and fleet of foot, which means understanding how to change/transform becomes an important capability.

So, what will successful, adaptive organizations look like over the next decade and beyond?

An ongoing sense of urgency

The internal rate of urgency needs to be high if the external competitive environment is changing fast. The idea that we will get long periods of calm or complacency punctuated by shorter periods of disruption doesn't look or feel realistic in today or tomorrow's business environment.

A high rate of urgency does not mean a constant state of panic, anxiety or fear. It means a state where complacency is absent, in which people are always scanning the horizon and reviewing issues and opportunities. The driver of much of this will be distributed data. The idea that only those at the very top of the organization should see all the data is clearly one area of change. Honest, open and regular data on customers, competitors, employees, supplies, stakeholders, technological developments and financial information should be available to all those who want it and can legitimately use it to improve organizational performance. This requires great transparency and trust, which are best developed by doing them; provide data to your people, ask for their help to improve the business. Trust is something that is built over time, but when in place enables organizations to be fleet of foot and able to change direction when the market or customers require it to.

Leadership is a team game

In a fast-moving world teamwork is essential. Individuals, however gifted or talented, won't be able to sift through all the data available and make sense of it. Teams are always essential in times of change. One change I can foresee is the selection of whole leadership teams, rather than individuals, becoming more commonplace as teams become recognized as the core drivers of increased value. Leadership succession will become much more about the team than the individual leader.

We can only hope that we get better at selecting leaders without gigantic egos. We need to continue to use 360 degree feedback and other feedback processes, so we help select leaders who can lead, change and take people with them. We will also require leaders who take a longer-term view and don't focus on the next quarter's results and their own tenure and rewards.

Leaders who communicate change

The ability to communicate strategy and vision are now so much more important than planning, budgeting, organizing and fixing problems. The ability to transform requires leaders to talk, engage, communicate and empower, which are all at the heart of people-centric transformation. Without enough leaders who are change orientated, transformation will just not happen well enough or fast enough to satisfy organizations needs and expectations. People look to leaders for many things; for decisions, permission and feedback. If your leaders behave the same way your people will see the transformation as a fad. Leaders who want to operate differently will need to master their ego, quieten their voice, get out of the way and become a coach. The leader's job is to ensure that the conditions for change are in place; they will be doing less traditional leadership activity and more creating and engaging.

Empower the people

In turbulent times, organizations need more of their people fully engaged and committed. We need to facilitate this with flatter hierarchies, less bureaucracy and a greater willingness to take risks. Yet again, leaders who delegate and empower, who trust their people to do the right thing will be well positioned for success. I am not sure we will need as many day-to-day managers to control the work as we move more towards self-managing teams who have objectives set by organizational leaders.

Adaptive culture

Cultures can facilitate adaptation if they have value creation and their customer at the centre, if the culture is supportive of competent leadership, if they encourage teamwork and minimum layers of bureaucracy. Truly adaptive firms with cultures that are also adaptive are awesome competitive machines. They produce great products/ services faster and better than traditional competitors. They run rings around bloated bureaucracies.

To create this type of culture you need to recognize that culture isn't a destination; it evolves over time. The point is that culture adapts to the changing world in which the business operates. You can help create this type of culture by prototyping and reframing experiments to ensure learning is captured and your people feel safe to try new things. However, failure needs to be recognized as ok, so learning is built upon. It's also important that difficult issues are discussed openly, and solutions sought from across the organization.

From here to there

The argument against transformation and change, which by its nature is disruptive and to some extent risky, is that organizations can survive or even succeed with incremental change. A 3 per cent improvement here and a 6 per cent cost reduction there will enable the business to win. In the short run and in certain industries this could be true. But my instinct, which the data also suggests, is that the competitive winners will be those that look for and take advantage of change, who can spot market opportunities and then create an offering to satisfy customers' needs they didn't know they had. That's an adaptive, agile organization with the ability to change at pace.

CHANGE AND TRANSFORMATION CHECKLIST

1 Review previous transformation or large-scale change programmes in your organization. Did they work? Were the planned benefits delivered? If not, what would you do differently next time?

2 Recognize change and transformation is context specific. Be very clear on the quest and the difference you want to make; this needs to be measurable. Don't forget the three key questions from Chapter 2: Why? What difference? How do we measure it?

3 Don't just focus on structural change; seek to make your transformation process multifaceted. This amplifies the chance of success.

4 Ensure your transformation programme includes hard and soft change and don't forget to tell your people what will remain the same.

5 Don't get sucked into one metaphor for the change. Seek to use different narratives/stories so people 'buy in'.

6 Always ensure purpose and meaning are at the heart of the transformational process.

7 Recognize the difference between change and transformation. Use the five strategies defined in this chapter to test your thinking.

8 When designing your transformation programme, ensure you use the four pillars:

   a. waking up the organization;

   b. ideas and vision;

   c. building support;

   d. implementing change.

9 The HR/people function should be at the centre of any transformational process, provided they have the skill and capability. If not, get outside help fast.

10 Recognize that becoming an adaptive organization means being able to change the organization system at pace and being able to course correct. Both help to create competitive advantage.

References

Anand, N and Barsoux, J-L (2017) What everyone gets wrong about change management, *Harvard Business Review* https://hbr.org/2017/11/what-everyone-gets-wrong-about-change-management

BBC News (2005) Royal Mail delivers record profit, 17 May http://news.bbc.co.uk/1/hi/business/4553933.stm

Bock, L (2015) *Work Rules: Insights from inside Google that will transform how you live and lead*, John Murray

De Geus, A (1999) *The Living Company: Growth, learning and longevity in business*, Nicholas Brealy

Drucker, PF (1999) *Management Challenges for the 21st Century*, Butterworth Heinemann

Gallup (nd) The Engaged Workplace www.gallup.com/services/190118/engaged-workplace.aspx

Kotter, JP (1996) *Leading Change*, Harvard Business School Press

Mirvis, P, Ayas, K and Roth, G (2003) *To the Desert and Back: The story of one of the most dramatic business transformations on record*, Jossey-Bass

Morgan, G (1993) *Imaginization: The art of creative management*, Sage
PWC (2018) Will robots really steal our jobs? PwC
Riddertråle, J and Nordström, K (2004) *Karaoke Capitalism: Management for mankind*, Pearson Education
Taffinder, P (1998) *Big Change: A route map for corporate transformation*, John Wiley & Sons
Teerlink, R and Ozley, L (2000) *More Than a Motorcycle: The leadership journey at Harley-Davidson*, Harvard Business School Press

09

Great people management

At the core of a Competitive People Strategy are your managers. Do they inspire, motivate, develop and get the most from your people? At the heart of delivering a great employee experience, creating a great culture or taking people through transformation, is the day-to-day leadership of people.

Most of this book is focused on the strategic leadership of people. However, we know that people's relationship with their manager and team is critical to how they perform. Many would argue that front-line managers are the most important component in a progressive people strategy. It's no secret that a good manager makes the difference in how happy and productive both teams and individuals are. Great managers have a positive multiplier effect on performance even in a people-centric business.

The employee's relationship with their manager has a direct correlation with their engagement and makes a major contribution to their perception of the organization. If employees can see the bigger picture, which takes a lot of managers' time to continuously explain, we know that they then feel a stronger connection to the company and its customers. Great managers excel at delegation, coaching and giving feedback. However, to do these well they have to understand people and be able to adapt their approach based on an assessment of the situation and knowing the character and personality of each of their people. Management is both an art and a science.

We covered leadership in Chapter 4, which was more about those with strategic people and organizational responsibilities. This chapter is focused on frontline managers; those who directly manage the majority of your people. They may be called team leaders, managers or even co-ordinators. What is common is they directly manage teams and individuals.

In Sam Walker's fantastic book *The Captain Class* (Walker, 2017), he concludes after an 11-year study of 1,200 teams across the world in 37 different sports that just one factor drives a winning collective effort, not a range of different indicators, as most believed. His research has revealed one simple yet powerful truth that can be applied in any other field including business, politics, science or the arts. The single most crucial ingredient in a sports team that achieves and sustains greatness is the character of the player who leads it.

Why people follow

One of the most important questions in people management success is 'Are your managers the type and calibre that people want to follow?' People have to want to voluntarily follow a manager. This demonstrates that management is not about being given a role or a title; it's about deploying a set of behaviours that earn people's respect and trust, creating a willingness to follow. Effective managers recognize that people must feel confident in the direction the manager and organization are heading and feel they want to follow. For people to have this level of confidence, the manager must be able to communicate their expectations and desired outcomes and then work with individuals and teams on how these can be achieved. Effective managers empower and enable people and teams to do their part in accomplishing the businesses' objectives.

It is very clear what followers want from their manager and leaders:

- genuine concern for their team;
- being a good communicator/networker and achiever;
- trusts others to lead;
- honest and consistent;

- accessible, approachable and flexible;
- decisive and ready to take risks;
- a shared vision.

(Wilkinson, 2015)

The behaviour of managers: The magic eight

These are the behaviours that, from experience, create effective, productive and high-performing teams and individuals.

1 Great provider of feedback and coaching
Employees value and appreciate a manager who takes the time to coach and help them learn. Being confident to give unsolicited feedback and praise is a core ability of good people managers. Managers must also be willing and able to provide difficult feedback when mistakes have occurred. In such instances, the framing of the feedback is important, and they need to be able to give specific examples and provide insight in how to avoid them happening again.

Coaching requires one essential ingredient that cannot be taught; caring not just about the tasks' completion, but also for the person being coached. The focus of a good coaching relationship is learning. A great manager facilitates the learning of their people. The role of coaching was first established in the world of sport and over time has proved indispensable in getting the best performance from individuals and teams who were already competent. Managers who coach well know the golden rule that what a person hears is more important than what the speakers says, and recognizes that there are often big differences between the two.

2 Work on team cohesion and performance
Line managers who add the most value are those that don't just improve individual performance, but also that of their team. We know that effective teams will always outperform even great individuals, regardless of their talent. If you have ever been part of a high-performing team you will immediately recognize why. You

share data and insight with one another because you have a common goal. You will also seek to problem solve and generate new ways of delivering value collectively. When teams work really well, they produce so much more than any of the team could contribute as individuals. Somehow being part of a well-functioning team creates energy, creativity and innovation. The leader has three clear roles in creating an effective team:

a. First, get the right people on the team, and try to get the right blend of skills, attitudes and diverse experience.

b. Second, the leader needs to create a clear strategy, a common goal for the team. Effective managers also allow the team the space to agree how they will achieve the team's goal. The leader should ensure the team gets to know each other well and that they spend time working on issues collectively.

c. Third, great teamwork takes practice and needs to be encouraged and nurtured. The manager needs to act as a sounding-board and team coach but always with a clear eye on the achievement of the end result.

3 Empowers and enables

Micromanaging is a common mistake of new managers who, without realizing it, undermine their own position and the performance of the team. The evidence is clear that people need to feel in control of their work and have a certain level of autonomy to perform at their best. They want to make decisions relevant to their own job. Great managers get the balance right between freedom and providing advice; they show trust but also show support and advocate for their team. The ability to effectively delegate while also providing support when needed is an attribute of an effective manager.

4 Goal setting

Effective people managers want to achieve results but recognize their job is to do this via other people. They possess the ability to translate business objectives into SMART goals for their team and the individuals that work for them. This provides clarity for the team and alignment for the organization. Great managers are able to explain how the achievement of their teams work and local goals will help the business achieve its overall objective. This creates an understanding amongst employees that their job matters and that what they do makes a difference. If managed well, this establishes a linkage between your people's daily activity and the organization's purpose. This creates meaning, which has been proven to improve both individual and team productivity.

5   **Communication skills**
In addition to providing feedback and setting goals, effective managers are excellent communicators. This means being able to both listen and speak well. How good are your managers at this core skill? Being a great listener means putting the speaker at ease, removing distractions and paying attention to non-verbal communication, such as eye contact and body language. Being good at speaking is all about two things – preparation and practice. Getting regular feedback from your employees on the effectiveness of their managers' communication skills either via a staff survey or 360 degree feedback mechanism is a good way to provide data and feedback to your managers on this critical skill. It's also a skill that can be easily learned and developed with practice.

6   **Focus on strengths rather than weaknesses**
Even today, with all the evidence available, the majority of managers still focus on providing feedback; examples and evidence of what their people are not good at. This obsession with helping people rectify their weaknesses is counter-productive. The focus of every great people manager is to concentrate on what someone is already good at and make them even better. Organizations need to capitalize on the capabilities their people possess, so the role of the manager is to help each person become more of who they already are. If people have developed a skill at which they are great, it nearly always follows that they enjoy doing this activity; build on what is already available. Ensure that your managers don't waste their time and effort trying to put in what was left out but instead make the most of the skill and talent already available to them and the organization.

7   **Recognize people are different**
Great people managers understand their people and are tuned in to how they are feeling. They also know where each of their team is in their own development journey, what they find easy and what

is difficult for them. This enables managers to react to situations with the right response for each individual. For example, the same individual may require direct feedback on one issue because they are experienced but have just lost focus, but may require a more supportive coaching approach on another issue because they are new to this activity. The manager should have a range of approaches that they can deploy, dependent on the situation and the individual's experience. This requires management agility and the ability to recognize the right response to each situation. This is the part of people management that takes time to develop; it can be taught but it requires lots of real-life experience to master.

8 Invest more time in your talent

Many managers assume that they should treat their team and every individual the same. The assumption is that anyone can be anything they want to be if they just try hard enough and get access to training and development. In fact, many organizations expect their managers to devise rules and policies to control employees' unruly inclinations and to fix the traits they lack! We don't use this language, but we informally tell our managers to either muzzle or correct what nature provided. The managers who make the most of the talent available recognize that each person is motivated differently; that they have their own way of thinking, seeing the world and relating to others. They recognize there is a limit to the remodelling and change they can create so they don't bemoan these differences; they embrace and utilize them. Managers must treat people fairly and all staff should be clear about the expectations the organization has of them, receiving coaching, feedback and development. However, great managers can get those with ability to add even more value by focusing on their strengths and seeking to make the most of them. The time and input might be similar but great managers get differentiated outcomes or results by focusing on building on their team's strengths.

If you can hire, develop and retain managers that have the eight behaviours defined above, you have the raw material to deliver on your Competitive People Strategy. The core role of people managers is simple; they need to hire well, ie select good people. They should set clear expectations for both individuals and teams, motivate each person and develop everyone who works for them. These four activities, if focused on with the behaviours described above, will enable your managers to outperform most of your competitors. It doesn't matter if your managers have vision, charisma and intelligence by the bucket load, if they cannot perform these eight activities they will never excel, and your organization will struggle to deploy its Competitive People Strategy.

Managers and leaders are not the same

There is a famous quote by Warren Bennis that says: 'managers do things right, while leaders do the right things' (Bennis and Nanus, 2007). This traditional view casts the manager as a dependable 'doer' while leaders are strategic and sophisticated. This view demeans what great people managers do for the business every day. It also often leads to managers being rebranded as leaders. However, leaders and managers should be focused on different activities. Great managers look inwards, a bit like a football coach; they seek to make the most of what they have. They seek to strengthen the team by hiring more talent, but they aim to motivate their team to perform to their full potential. Whereas leaders look outwards at a football club; think of the Chief Executive who is thinking about the brand, marketing and sales as well as the customers wants and needs. They focus on broad patterns and trends and seek to find areas of competitive advantage. These are two very different skill sets. Great managers are not 'mini' or developing leaders, and great leaders are not simply managers who have got an MBA and can now strategize!

If companies confuse or conflate the two roles by expecting every manager to be a leader, or they think of leaders as just more sophisticated managers, the core activities of managers will be undervalued and not focused upon, with disastrous consequences for both the delivery of your Competitive People Strategy and, ultimately, your business results.

Attracting great people managers

Businesses are beginning to recognize the importance of their frontline staff to overall business outcomes. Delivering a great employee experience and fully engaged people is dependent on having great people managers. The behaviour defined above (the Magic Eight) should be used as the criteria against which to select managers. Having great managers is commercially important; hiring talented people to manage the workforce can create a long-term competitive advantage all on its own as they can attract great people, motivate them to perform, create great teams and retain the people the business needs. However, the majority of organizations don't spend enough time on hiring or developing frontline managers. Most organizations, for the last decade, have focused on leadership development. This is important; however, leaders can define any business strategy they like but if they don't have people managers who can inspire and motivate the people to execute it... well, it's all hot air!

Hire the right people managers

Getting the right people in frontline management roles is critical to the implementation of an effective people strategy, yet this important task receives little focus in most business strategies or even within HR functions. The view of many is that managing people is 'not rocket science'. However, organizations should look for great people managers with the same amount of vigour, preparation and dedication as if they were hiring rocket scientists! They make a huge difference. These managers are responsible for the asset that creates a massive proportion of your business value – your people. This is the most important job in any organization. As part of your people strategy, ensure it is given enough attention, resource and focus.

In Chapter 6 we explored moving away from a dependence on interviews alone in selection. Here are a few additional ideas on how to ensure you are selecting the right people for line management roles:

- Be creative. Every candidate will be prepared for the standard interview questions. Get behind the process and seek to get to know the whole person.

- Be challenging. Put the candidate in real-life situations where they are not comfortable and where they will have to demonstrate how they would tackle the issue if appointed. You see their true selves in these situations.

- Get others involved. The boss of the line manager is not the only one who will have to work with the appointed candidate. There is likely to already be a team of employees that you can trust to be part of the process and who can have an important perspective in the selection process.

- Take them on a tour of the office. This has always proved to be worthwhile in any recruitment/selection process. Take your candidate around the company and introduce them to some of their potential colleagues. The things to pay attention to are:

    Are they interested in the work and the people? Do they ask sensible questions about what people are doing (the work) and ask questions about the people themselves?

    Are they curious? Do they follow up initial questions with those that show they are genuinely interested?

    Do they treat everyone, regardless of role, with respect?

The tour should be an essential part of the selection process for people managers. You could also include a meal with two peers (current good-performing line managers) as part of the selection process once you are down to two or three potential candidates. This not only provides the candidates with a great opportunity to ask questions and get beneath the surface of the organization, but it also enables your line managers to watch and observe the behaviour of the candidate. Things they should observe are:

- Are they polite to everyone who is serving them? Do they look people in the eye?

- Are they irritated or flustered by the real-life experiences of the problems they might encounter if they were appointed to the role?
- Can they keep the conversation going? Are they easy to get along with? Are they interested in what is being said?
- Do they listen well? Do they ask thoughtful follow-up questions based on the insight provided?

This process, along with the more formal assessment centre described in the earlier chapter, allows you the opportunity to see the candidate's personality; it's a microcosm of life.

We all have bias and it's important that these are challenged when hiring people managers. Competency bias is often a problem for hiring managers. We are biased towards competency because we are conditioned to focus on 'CV virtues'. We tend to use status or other extrinsic markers like wealth, titles, previous experience, awards, accolades and even social media followings as indicators for determining people's competence. Whereas, we recommend seeking opportunities to see beyond what is written in the CV. Let's see how they really relate to people and deal with realistic and, on occasions, difficult situations.

Appointing a first-time manager

The appointment of someone who has never managed people before is a critical organizational decision. We need to recognize it is not just about selection, but also about how we develop and get new managers up to speed. The amount of times very capable managers have described to me the way in which they were thrown in at the deep end early in their managerial career is truly frightening. These hires are high risk because, while you may have good knowledge about the individual (if they are internal candidates), they won't have managed others before. Appointing external candidates to a line manager's role who has no management experience is even more risky because at least with an internal candidate you will have lots of relevant information about their performance to date. The importance of an assessment centre and the testing of candidates for managerial roles cannot be stressed enough. Assessment centres provide a great opportunity for those that have not led teams before to demonstrate their ability. Also, if this is done with others who are experienced managers, you will get a very clear picture of their innate ability. However, it is essential that people appointed to people management roles get robust, effective onboarding. You want to ensure your new managers understand the context and get a good handle on the team quickly. This helps them perform well in their role. First-time managers need even more support and hand-holding. Mistakes will be made; that's part of the learning process, but they need effective feedback and coaching so they reflect and learn how to handle difficult situations and different personalities effectively.

Developing great people management

It is important that those that manage your people are developed so that they are excellent. This starts with the onboarding process, where expectations are defined and basic information is provided. There should then be more formal training and development interventions where first-time managers and those that are new to your organization can practise and develop the core skills in a safe environment with lots of feedback.

We may need to go even further by providing mentoring and coaching, as both are highly effective at growing confidence, skill and capability.

Mentoring

Mentoring is a broader relationship than coaching as it provides counselling, a sounding board and support for new managers. This can be provided in-house by an experienced line manager, or more effectively by an experienced manager in another non-competitive business. Mentoring is a longer-term relationship than coaching; it provides listening and advice in a non-judgemental way. Mentors provide advice and practical experience along with information. They also seek to role model and create opportunities to work with the mentee on specific issues or challenges they have.

Coaching

This aims to enhance the performance and learning ability of those being coached. It involves the coach giving feedback, but it also includes other techniques such as effective questioning; it is a dynamic interaction where the coach encourages reflection and learning. This helps those being coached to become more self-aware and it develops the practical skills required by those who are asked to manage others.

Managing teams

Most line managers have to manage a team of people as well as a set of individuals. However, when you look at the huge amount of published material on management, the bulk of it is focused on managing and developing individuals. Also, if you think of your organizations HR processes, policies and procedures in relation to people, they are all, yes all, related to the individual. Yet we know that great performance is predominantly delivered by teams and not by individuals. We need to create a new set of tools and much greater emphasis on how to create and manage team performance. Managers' ability to communicate and develop a relationship with all the members of their team is critical for building trust, promoting collaboration and enhancing teamwork. The skills associated with managing a team successfully include:

- Assemble the right team: Assembling a team who enjoy working with each other is an important contributor to team success. When selecting people to join your team or assessing the current team, you should be reviewing both technical skills and behaviour, eg communication, listening, empathy and drive. When selecting team members, testing not only ensures they have the skills to contribute but also that they will fit into the team so that overall team performance is improved.

- Trust the team to do the job: managers should delegate well and avoid micromanaging, as this is seen by most as intrusive and demonstrates a lack of trust in the team. However, offering support when individuals and the team are under pressure or struggling is also important; it's all about balance.

- Consistency: This is also a matter of balance. The team leader needs to take into consideration the different skill levels and personality of team members when deciding how to manage. The manager needs to have a diversity of approaches when managing a team. They need to leave the correct amount of space, so people don't feel cramped while also providing support when it is needed. This can be difficult, as the manager needs to be seen to be managing the team both consistently and fairly. The same behaviour needs to be recognized and rewarded by the manager so that the team have a clear view of what is expected of them individually and collectively.

- Celebrate success: If the team or individual has done a good job, the manager should publicly acknowledge it. This recognition develops a relationship based on appreciation of the effort the team are putting in. Again, this needs to be delivered in a consistent manner.

- Focus on a common goal: On top of their own individual targets, a good manager will ensure there is an overriding team target, so the team succeed or fail together. This creates unity; it helps improve communication and it encourages support and collaboration. Being an effective manager means creating a positive environment where the team problem-solve and resolve issues themselves.

- Communication: The manager should communicate information to the team while also facilitating good communication within the team. Everyone should know what is going on. However, a great manager also spends time creating an environment of open feedback, so the team can question priorities and plan activity together. Two-way communication solidifies trust.

- Foster development: Identifying both individual and team learning needs is an important managerial capability. The team should provide coaching and feedback to one another. Upskilling and training the team is a great way to encourage people to give their best. The organization and manager should help people master new skills, which is proven to help retain talent. The team also needs to develop together, so regular opportunities to build the team and spend time learning from each other is important. Team building should be a regular activity.

Fewer or no managers

Many businesses are asking 'Do we need managers at all?' If we get data from outside and inside the organization, can't teams make their own decisions and execute them without the need for a manager at all? This concept questions the historic role of managers, which was to organize, control and ensure work happened, which we agree is now much less important.

What is clear is we require people who have the capability to engage and influence the way employees feel about themselves, their work and the organization they work for. Additionally, we need to help teams work effectively with technology. This will include how to work with algorithms that solve problems, learn and provide creative answers to customer issues. This means people and technology working together so data, logic and emotion are all fully utilized. The ability to obtain the most from people and AI is where most organizations will be going in the next few years. However, the role of the manager will remain important in the next decade. The ability to coach, develop, innovate and create collaboration will be even more critical to business success. The manager will move from being seen as an overhead, to a provider of value to both individuals and teams by supporting people's development, creating clarity of purpose and optimizing team performance.

GREAT PEOPLE MANAGEMENT CHECKLIST

1 Review how strong (well-developed) your frontline managers are. Look at data from employee surveys and 360 degree feedback. If you don't have data, then doing some specific anonymous surveys will provide an insight into where you are.

2 Review your line manager selection criteria and development activity against the magic eight management behaviours.

3 Review your selection process for frontline people managers. Are you robustly testing not just their skills, but also their behaviour and attitude?

4 Validate your approach to appointing new managers. Ensure you have a robust onboarding process.

5 Develop a coaching and mentoring programme for new managers so that you are fully developing their management capability quickly and effectively.

6 Generate a team development playbook with a set of tools and approaches on how to create, nurture and develop a high-performing team.

7 Map the development of your managers as you start to automate work and make sure they can develop an integrated human/AI team. Line managers of the future are going to have to be able to utilize data, technology and people to optimize performance.

References

Argyris, C (1991) Teaching smart people to learn the inner game of work, *Harvard Business Review*

Bennis, WG and Nanus, B (2007) *Leaders: The strategies for taking charge*, HarperCollins

Buckingham, M (2005) What great managers do, *Harvard Business Review*

Buckingham, M and Coffman, C (1999) *First Break all the Rules: What the world's greatest managers do differently*, Simon and Schuster

Gallwey, T (2000) *Overcoming Mental Obstacles for Maximum Performance*, Orion

Katzenbach, JR and Smith, DK (1993) The discipline of teams, *Harvard Business Review*

Malone, TW (2004) *The Future of Work: How the new order of business will shape your organization, your management style and your life*, Harvard Business School Press

Margretta, J with Stone, N (2002) *What Management Is: How it works and why it's everyone's business*, Profile

Mauri, T (2017) *The Leader's Mindset: How to win in the age of disruption*, Terence Mauri

Pink, DH (2009) *Drive: The surprising truth about what motivates us*, Canongate

Walker, S (2017) *The Captain Class: The hidden force that creates the world's greatest teams*, Penguin

Wilkinson, P (2015) *The Dependent Organization*, Brown Dog

10

Developing the people function

Designing and executing a Competitive People Strategy

The HR profession has not evolved in the last two decades and certainly not at the same pace as the business environment. In 1997, David Ulrich in his book *HR Champions* pioneered a new focus and structure for the HR profession. However, since this seminal text, the HR function has not innovated or reimagined how it undertakes its work. There are, of course, some HR functions and many HR practitioners who have sought to add more value to their organizations and the people that work within them. However, to deliver the agenda espoused in this book, the HR profession has a moment of truth; either it ups its game or I believe others will take responsibility for strategic people activity, leaving the HR function as an operational delivery unit. The HR profession is now at a tipping point as the world of work changes at a faster pace than ever before.

Why HR needs to up its game

Organizations are no more than a collection of people brought together to achieve a common aim or goal. It has become apparent over the last decade that human capital (people) are now the key drivers of business success. It's people and teams who innovate, develop new brands and who seek to deepen relationships with customers and utilize new technology. It's now people that make the difference between business success and failure. However, when you observe the behaviour of organizations, the vast majority behave just as businesses did in the early 20th century. They still predominantly focus on shareholder value, efficiency, effectiveness and cost reduction. While helpful in delivering short-term improvement in financial performance, these behaviours will not deliver long-term sustainable value. Successful businesses are unique in that they are better at responding to customers' wants and needs than their competitors. This point of difference often gets lost as an organization grows and inherently becomes more complex. As part of developing a Competitive People Strategy, businesses must seek to align their people to the core value that they are providing for customers. The customers are the people who pay our wages, after all. This links the people to the organization's purpose and strategy. The evidence is emphatic; the more people understand and buy into why the organization exists, the more the people are engaged and motivated. The evidence also proves that a great employee experience leads to improved productivity and performance.

Observations about HR as it is today

I've spent a large amount of time over the last year reading about HR and, just as importantly, talking to HR leaders and their teams. I've also sought out feedback from MDs, CEOs and other business leaders. The views I outline below are mine, but they have been informed by this investigative process:

- HR still thinks top-down; we design people policies, processes and procedures because we are the experts and we know best.

- We don't treat our people as individuals; we don't tailor our products or services to their individual requirements, wants or needs. They just get what they are given!

- We focus on consistency as a mechanism to ensure fairness when, in fact, we may need different interventions for different parts of the business.

- HR seek to implement good practice rather than develop a differentiated offering. This is the complete opposite of the competitive behaviour recommended in this book, which is to seek to provide a people strategy that is better than, not the same as, our competitors.

- We still work on a rule- or permission-based model. We design processes because we think that without them our people won't do the right thing. The classic example of this is performance management. If there wasn't a process, managers wouldn't set objectives, review performance or provide feedback. Really?

- We don't use data or deep insight to help us diagnose and then plan people interventions. We rarely define the outcomes we are seeking to achieve for those interventions, so it's difficult to show we have succeeded, but also, we never fail! We focus on the inputs (process and policy) rather than the business outcomes.

- We are overloaded and sometimes overwhelmed by the volume of work; we don't stop activity we just keep adding initiatives without eliminating what doesn't add value.

- We have too few people who are commercially minded enough to design interventions with measurable business benefit.

- We spend far too much time and effort on the tactical matters and too little time on those that are of strategic or commercial importance.

- We seek to ensure compliance to internal processes that often have been over-designed, to avoid any risk taking. We seek to design out non-conformity, but in fact by doing this we eliminate creativity and innovation.

- We are over-zealous in our focus on individuals, yet more value could be added with a greater focus on team performance and culture.

However, there is a huge opportunity for the people function to add value:

- Remove bureaucracy and systems where they do not add value and stifle progress. HR needs to become a 'red tape' buster!

- Focus on leadership by developing, hiring and growing capability across our organizations.

- Seek to take a differentiated view of what we offer and focus on. How are we better than our competitors? Are we better at hiring critical capability, retaining a higher percentage of talent, growing leaders and talent at a faster rate, getting better performance from our customer-facing teams, or do we have the best sales function in the industry?

- Co-create people products and services with our managers and people.

- Involve our people in creating new ideas and ways of working so we improve every day.

- Deploy Lean and Agile methodologies in a thoughtful manner so we are constantly looking to do things more efficiently while becoming more innovative.

- Measure how well we deliver HR services and products. Seek to make HR just work. We should make people processes easy and simple for managers and our people to use.

- Design every intervention with a clear, measurable outcome in mind. Capture data on our own delivery performance and seek to improve it.

- Focus more on organization and team performance than on individuals. Provide more support, development and guidance to managers about optimizing team performance, because the majority of work is delivered by teams, not individuals.

Technology: Help and hindrance

The world of business is very different from when I first started work in 1979. Everything then was paper-based. We had computers, but these were awkward and rudimentary in nature. The computers were in a huge sealed room, which was the domain of the few computer staff. The fax machine was a way of improving communication, but in reality this was just photocopying between organizations. The internet was not even talked about by academics or futurologists! A mobile phone had a battery the size of a shoe box and weighed 20lbs.

The impact of technology on work over the last 20 years has been profound but I don't think we have seen anything yet! This will only accelerate over the next decade. These developments will have huge implications for the jobs of the future. Every developed economy has been losing jobs in the middle of their labour market, and this will accelerate. There has been a very significant growth in high-paid, high-skilled jobs, and also in low-paid, low-skilled jobs. However, the jobs in the middle of organizations have been eliminated in increasing numbers. Routine administrative work has been removed by a ceaseless drive for greater efficiency and effectiveness. The competitive pressure on organizations to create value and at the same time to be highly efficient is growing. In fact, all the evidence suggests that AI, machine learning, IOT and 3D printing will move away from just automating routine administrative roles into replacing repeatable cognitive work that until recently we thought would never be undertaken by computers.

The impact of this technological change on work and business cultures will have both positive and negative effects. Many of the jobs that will be eliminated are boring, routine and repetitive. The internet and mobile communication have enabled organizations to become faster, more dynamic and responsive to customer needs. The ability to communicate in real time with anyone else on the planet has empowered consumers and helped businesses both small and large to operate with a global footprint. However, this has bought huge amounts of organizational change, often creating workplace cultures that are overly demanding, stressful and, in some instances, harmful.

The Ulrich Model

The HR function has been struggling to keep up with the relentless pace of change. The Three Box or Ulrich Model first talked about in the late 1990s (Ulrich, 1997) has recently come in for criticism.

However, we must not forget where the profession was before this new approach to HR. We were still operating as a personnel function, much as we had been for the preceding 50 years. The idea that HR had many different roles to play was fresh, innovative and new in 1997. It helped the HR function rapidly move away from doing what it had always done, to thinking about itself as a real deliverer of organizational value. The concept that you can improve the delivery of HR services by creating a technology enabled shared service with an improved employee experience still has merit. Second, the idea that we needed to be more proactive in our work with business leaders and become true partners was long overdue. The third concept was that HR had important expertise in reward, learning, OD and talent that could impact on business performance. This enabled a more focused approach on the development of HR expertise and specialism that had not been deployed before Ulrich's seminal work. Therefore, on reflection, the Ulrich Three Box Model was a significant development in the history of people management. It improved the delivery of HR and allowed the function to play a more meaningful role within our organizations. However, the function now seems to be trapped, with little innovation since the 1990s. The time is now right for HR to reinvent itself for the next decade.

Why we need to change

Over the last 20 years, HR has not focused enough time and energy on thinking about how we respond to the growing significance of people to competitive success. HRDs and CPOs have not had the bandwidth to reposition themselves or the HR function as the true deliverers of performance improvement and innovation.

Second, the majority of HR business partners are just not providing the value that we all originally envisaged. They have become obsessed about managing and improving the relationship with business leaders they partner with, rather than defining strategic interventions for business benefit. They often spend time ensuring that the HR shared service centre are doing what they should, often resolving individual employee issues on a daily basis. They regularly pull in experts from centres of excellence who, on occasion, are far too removed from the business to provide meaningful interventions. The experts are seeking to do good work and design organization-wide interventions, but often from a conceptual good practice perspective rather than being co-creators of value with line managers and human resource business partners (HRBPs). The HRD or CPO is then left to try to make the tripartite HR function work across the business, while also being the CEO's business partner!

What's next?

The shared service and HR business partners need to be reintegrated so they function as one HR delivery or operational unit. This will provide greater responsiveness and an enhanced manager and employee experience. The experts or centres of excellence should be recrafted to go far beyond the traditional HR disciplines and become champions of organizational transformation, technology deployment and strategic leaders of change management programmes. The CPO/ HRD needs to be rebranded as the organizations people strategist or architect. This isn't about just changing the name; it's about crafting new capability.

Does the most senior people executive need to own the HR operational function? The people strategist or architect should support the CEO and leadership team with strategic analysis on people transformation, leadership and organizational development. This is a significant opportunity for the HR function to evolve. We have a moment of truth, where we either reinvent ourselves or organizations will look to others to play the strategic people/transformational role.

In partnership with LACE Partners (a HR transformation consultancy), I have recently undertaken a research project on the future of HR, called *HR on the Offensive* (LACE Partners, 2019). The project had two objectives. First, to explore where the HR function is today and secondly, how should it evolve? The research threw up many innovative ideas and demonstrated that the size of the opportunity for HR to make more of an impact on commercial success is huge. At the end of this chapter I've produced a checklist of questions for HR or business leaders to use when reviewing their HR function.

1. HR structures and stages of maturity

Each business chooses its own strategy and operating model. These both have a huge impact on how HR is structured and how it adds value. This was evident from the research with businesses, both globally and in the United Kingdom. Organizations with a small head office function and a federated operational model (with strong regional or sector specific structure) tended to have an HR function with a very similar dispersed model.

These types of dispersed businesses tend not to use a shared service, are lightly resourced at the centre and have a generalist model. To some extent they are still operating in a pre-Ulrich world. All of those we interviewed were in the process of exploring different ways of operating the HR function so it delivered greater business benefit. In some situations, it may be easier to change from this position than those that have been using the Ulrich model for some time. A great example of this was one international distribution company, which employed 20,000 people, but only had 10 people in group HR, had no shared service and no common HR system.

> 'We are very federal. The focus is on devolved accountability with regional MDs having full accountability. So the HR structure is similar with little light strategic guidance from the centre.'
>
> Julie Welch, Group HR Director, Bunzl (now Chief People Officer, Carey Group)

In our study, AB Sugar, Aggreko (whist they were reengineering the HR structure) and to some extent Veon PLC were all in the process of redesigning how they deliver HR in the future. They want to improve the capability of HR partners, leverage technology and become more strategically able. However, it cannot be stressed enough that a 'one size fits all' approach to the structure of HR will not work now, as it hasn't in the past. The structure of an HR function is much less important than defining a coherent people strategy and executing it well. How you resource the execution of your people strategy is very much secondary. Being clear on what you are doing and why is much more important than the HR structure that delivers it. It is worth reminding HR people sometimes that organizational structure is not a strategy!

The core finding of the LACE Partners research project is that a much higher number of businesses than we or the literature assumed have not yet gone to the Ulrich Three Box Model; as many as 25 per cent. So, while the HR profession should continue its ongoing debate about structure, the focus should move towards more analysis and evidence gathering so that Competitive People Strategies are created that assist their organizations to compete and win. These pre-Ulrich HR functions are often not using technology to leverage or add value. They don't have a structure or operating model that would justify the level of investment required to purchase a global HR system. It may not matter strategically because their federated or local model enables them to be close to customers and be nimble enough to deliver constantly.

The vast majority of business (75 per cent) who have implemented the Ulrich inspired Three Box Model had gone through two or three modifications over the last 15–20 years since they originally deployed the structure, but the majority had stuck with the core operating principles.

'We are in the early stages of an HR transformation. We will create shared service centres with standard ways of operating, upgrading to one global HR system, while investing in HR capability. We were operating sub-optimally. We now need HR to contribute so much more.'

Val Dale, Global HR Operations Director, Aggreko

2. Making the Three Box Model work

The LACE Partners research identified that HRBPs were not adding enough strategic value. It was apparent that HRBPs viewed the business relationship element of their role above all else. This often leads to them becoming subservient order-takers rather than true business partners. Ulrich had envisioned a true partner who jointly owned the people strategy with business leaders. It was apparent that the level of challenge to business leaders was often not visible. The ability of HR to hold up the mirror to the organization is a major partnering skill that many HRDs (65 per cent) said their business partners did not do robustly or effectively enough.

The relationship driver often leads HRBPs to become the customer service manager for the HR shared service centre, or even worse the fixer of every HR process that does not work. This remedial activity takes crucial resource away from impactful, strategic activity and reinforces the subservient nature of many HR business partners.

> 'We are starting to challenge line manager behaviour in a positive way as part of being more explicit about what people leaders need to do every day as a core part of their job.'
>
> Val Dale, Global HR Operations Director, Aggreko

The centres of excellence or HR experts were often described as ivory tower designers of solutions that should be closer to the business. Often, interventions were justified as being best practice. This leads to many interventions being poorly executed as business leaders often feel that they don't own the solution, and what is being imposed isn't fit for purpose. A move towards a co-creation or Agile approach to HR, product or service development would be a step in the right direction. If leaders and managers don't own people processes, policies or procedures, implementing them becomes difficult, hence why they often don't land well. Quite often, the relationship between HRBP and centres of excellence is ripe for improvement, with greater shared ownership for business outcomes an aspirational goal.

HR shared services are often perceived as just a back-office processing or support centre. Often, their focus could be best described as having at least one eye on unit costs or the cost to serve metric. The dominant mindset is one of cost efficiency above all else. These KPIs are far too focused on reducing cost per outcome. The ability of shared services to deliver a better employee and manager experience that has a positive impact on performance and productivity has been overlooked too often on the altar of efficiency. The opportunity to seize the shared service agenda is made much easier if employee and manager engagement is measured. You can develop user satisfaction or NPS data, which can then be used to rebalance the focus onto better delivery and employee experience rather than just cost efficiency. Shared services should aim to deliver 'HR that just works', as Laszlo Bock, HRD at Google, calls it (Bock, 2015). This would involve delivering the basics flawlessly every time. No errors in payroll or offer letters, bonuses paid on time with a clear explanation. Resourcing would have great candidates for every job, with fair and robust promotion processes and, most importantly, speedy resolution of employee issues or concerns. HR shared services should aspire to run a high-quality operation with an ongoing quest to improve the offering to staff based upon regular employee feedback.

> 'We [HR] have become leaner and more efficient, but are still predominantly doing the same or similar activity to 10 years ago.'
>
> Louise Wallwork, HR Director, BAE Systems Air Sector

Only 10 per cent of organizations that participated in the LACE Partners research had sought to go beyond the standard HR Ulrich operating model. A more flexible and involved approach to how HR is delivered should be an outcome of a Competitive People Strategy, not the precursor to it.

3. HR capability

The vast majority of HRDs in our research perceive their own HR function to be operating at market average capability. In the data collection process, only one organization gave any part of its HR function a score of 5 (our definition of market leading). This was the score AB Sugar gave its communities of practice (centres of excellence). While 75 per cent of organizations scored one part of HR as a 2 (low capability) the vast majority scored the HR function as a 3 (market average). This highlights the opportunity for most HR functions to make a significant step change in performance and contribution to organizational performance.

One solution to the challenge of improving HR capability is to improve the mix of talent within the people function. At present, a vicious cycle exists where the most talented and capable in our organizations shy away from HR because that's not where 'talent goes', or say it could be a 'dead end' in my career. In too many companies HR is full of nice people who work hard but don't deliver enough business value. It seems obvious, but HR should compete for the best talent more actively with other functions, whether marketing, sales, operations or finance. To do this, the 'HR' brand needs to be repositioned. We are crying out for leadership and one area our professional bodies could help would be to change the public perception of the HR function. Let's talk up what we do and the impact we make.

> 'Overall, the challenge for the function is to do three different things well all at the same time. First, provide a great employee experience. Second, create a great narrative so we win the hearts and minds of our workforce. Third, look for data on how we can improve performance.'
>
> Julie Welch, Group HR Director, Bunzl (now Chief People Officer, Carey Group)
>
> 'We've got to move away from process, policies and procedures towards innovative people strategies based on organizational design, capability planning, talent attraction and leadership development.'
>
> Jacky Symmonds, Chief People Officer, Veon

However, only 30 per cent of the HR functions who participated in the LACE Partners research had any strategic HR learning intervention in place. This would have been understandable if the HRDs were scoring their functions as above market average or market leading, but this wasn't the case. This is a huge omission and an obvious area for HRDs to invest in to get improved performance from the function.

HRBPs were by the far the most talked about part of HR. This, I believe, is because it's the business-facing part of HR and often drives the people agenda. The vast majority of the development activity, which was at best tactical and random, reinforces the opportunity to significantly up-skill the capability of the HR function. One HRD suggested that the core development process for HR practitioners five years into their career should include access to an external mentor (non-HRD) and participation in short, sharp retreats focused on different approaches to creating organizational success.

Here are some HR directors' views on the importance of the business partner role and how they believe these critical roles could make a greater contribution:

'HRBPs should be able to diagnose business problems and have the capability to design specific solutions. They need consulting and organizational development skills on steroids.'

Kathryn Pritchard, Group Chief People and Strategic Programmes Officer, Odeon

'The future requirement of HRBPs is to be able to work at a holistic and systemic level. This requires consultancy skills and deep business knowledge, as well as being a people process expert.'

Simon Linares, Group HR Director, Direct Line

'We've made a huge investment in our HRBPs. We're looking for and developing a growth mindset, analytical strength and a fair amount of resilience.'

Ralph Tribe, Group Chief People Officer, Ascential

HR needs to hire different capability. When I was an HRD, I aspired to have a strong mix of HR specialists, so that we had depth of people expertise, and leaders who had held senior line positions so they knew what people leadership on the ground was like and could articulate what would add value to managers and leaders. The third group were consultants, especially strategy (rather than HR) consultant because they had the analytical skills to diagnose problems and provide business solutions, while also having the ability to influence decisions. I would now add to that data and people analytics capability.

The conversations with many of the interviewees (HRDs) in the LACE Partners research project seemed to indicate that they believed they could grow their own HR capability and buy in additional expertise if they didn't have anyone job-ready to fill a vacancy. However, considering the shortage of talent available in the HR market, this seems an inadequate response to developing the HR function's most critical capability. Surely progressive HRDs should be developing and implementing strategic development programmes for their HRBPs. This seems a prerequisite of being able to execute a Competitive People Strategy so it can deliver on its own expectations and those of business leaders.

4. Measurement

The ability to use data is seen to be a critical future competence for any leading HR function. At present, the majority of HR functions are able to use only very basic people data.

There were three clear approaches to data and measurement that the HRDs in our study identified. The first was aligning people metrics to business or customer metrics (such as in the customer service–profit chain). This is a proven approach to assisting HR define its priorities, especially in consumer-focused businesses like Odeon, Bupa, Seven Trent and Veon.

The second approach was the desire to use data to achieve greater insight and to be able to design more targeted and effective people interventions and then measure their impact.

The third area, and by far the least developed, was that of predictive people analytics. Many of the HRDs (75 per cent) said that this was a major development opportunity for HR and one they believed, over time, they could utilize to provide greater business value

> 'We are a tightly regulated business so we have to focus on improving operational performance year after year. This means HR has to move away from blindly designing HR policies and procedures and become the champions of change, using data to deliver greater insight and better solutions.'
>
> Neil Morrison, HR Director, Severn Trent
>
> 'As a FTSE 250 company, we have all the normal HR compliance activity, but this doesn't really help us succeed. What is important is the right HR capability focused on data, evidence and insight. These enable us to make the right interventions and ultimately impact positively on business results.'
>
> Ralph Tribe, Group Chief People Officer, Ascential
>
> 'Our HR business partners are effective because they focus on data and evidence more than any other HR function I know. This allows us to challenge and then to co-create solutions with the line.'
>
> Ruth Smyth, Chief Talent Officer International, Publicis sapient

5. HR's self-image and confidence

One of the most surprising findings of this HR study was that, as well as hard HR expertise and commercial acumen, there was a growing need for HR professionals to have strong influencing skills. Many HRDs said that we needed to radically upgrade HR, with our mindset becoming more confident, assertive and sure of ourselves.

This was best articulated as a journey in which the HR profession has made significant progress over the last decade, but which still finds itself needing to up its game to fulfil its full potential. It also reflects the recognition by CEOs and other business leaders that the people (often articulated as talent) agenda is the driver of future business performance. There was deep frustration amongst HRDs who, while recognizing the progress, feel the profession is not moving at the speed necessary to respond to the leadership and market challenges. This mindset shift requires a range of changes to be made:

- HR needs to compete with other functions (marketing, finance and sales) for the brightest and best talent. We need to get the best raw material available.

- Create a different mix of capability in HR – bring in more experienced leaders, consultants, and data specialists.

- Develop what we have like never before, with a focus on business success.

- Create case studies and networks where people transformation is the focus so that people hear and see what 'good' looks like.

> 'We've got the focus of HR right here, now we just need to believe in ourselves and keep pushing. We've got to be more resilient.'
>
> Ruth Smyth, Chief Talent Officer International, Publicis Sapient

6. HR is too reactive

Another consistent theme of the LACE Partners research was that the whole people function provides what is requested or demanded rather what the business needs. This clearly builds on the earlier point about confidence and HRs mindset. However, it also raises the question 'Are HR business leaders or a support function?' Most thought that a significant shift was required so that business leaders saw heads of HR as peers and recognized HR as making a strategic contribution to organizational performance. Now is the time for the HR profession to lead a global debate (not just amongst those in HR but also in the wider business community) on the impact of dynamic and effectively executed people strategies that enable organizational success and make our businesses great places to work.

'HR often falls back to servicing the wants of our customers because it's comfortable and what we've always done. However, HR now needs to educate, challenge and develop leaders like never before so the business can thrive in tomorrow's marketplace.'

Louise Wallwork, HR Director, BAE Systems Air Sector

7. Developing leaders and managers

All HRDs in our research said they wanted to work with business leaders who truly recognized that it's people who deliver value to customers as well as managers who inspire, coach and motivate their people day in and day out. All the organizations were active in developing the manager population, but when asked to score the capability of their line managers, most again said they were average at best. Most felt that progress was being made but that again, in comparison to market disruption, they needed to intensify their efforts and build greater momentum. Some HRDs felt that the more managers see HR as being a force for creativity and innovation and less as the policeman of compliance, the more they will turn to HR for advice and guidance. Both Google and 3M give staff between 15 and 20 per cent of their time to work on their own projects (Goetz, 2011). Both believe that this develops organizational value through insight and problem solving. If the people function champions these types of employee innovations, then they will be recognized as facilitators of change and less as risk mitigators.

'We have to drive a more distributed model for leadership. HR has a critical role to ensure long-term business success by helping organizations and leaders build the capabilities and capacities they need to adapt to a rapidly changing environment.'

Louise Wallwork, HR Director, BAE Systems Air Sector

'We need to build managers' people skills at warp speed.'

Neil Morrison, HR Director, Severn Trent

8. Developing an outside view

One of the most refreshing and encouraging outcomes of the LACE Partners research was the recognition that HR professionals should be looking outside their own organization to learn and to think differently.

Many HRDs recognized the importance of seeking fresh perspectives from outside their own businesses that would stimulate their thinking and help with innovation. They were all keen to learn from others' experience. Seeking to create change with only your internal resource isn't going to cut it in the decade ahead. When asked how good they were at networking and going outside, 95 per cent said they and their teams needed to improve and find time to meet with customers, other businesses, suppliers and even competitors. What seems to hinder this is the ferocious and relentless workload of the HR function. This outside learning should be a large part of people practitioners' continuous personal development, but also an essential driver of competitive advantage. You have to keep benchmarking what is done.

> 'We need to look outside our own organizations. Do we really know what "great" looks like? We need to explore what others are doing because we don't know what we don't know.'
>
> Jacky Simmonds, Chief People Officer, Veon

9. The future of HR

We asked HRDs to articulate what they thought the future held for the HR profession. The vast majority described an urgent need to become more strategic, spending more time on organizational development, data, talent and culture. They recognized that too much resource and energy is currently focused on individuals. Some saw this as an opportunity to provide more value, but many recognized that HR needed greater capability, skill and a new focus to achieve this.

'In ten years' time HR will be somewhere or nowhere. We have to own our change; we must be tech-enabled, externally focused, data-driven and more deliberate, or it's over.'

Ralph Tribe, Chief People Officer, Ascential

10. People strategist/architect

Some of those who participated in the research suggested that the delivery of the vast majority of HR interventions (90 per cent) could be detached from a new people strategist/architect role. The views expressed by some were that HR could become two separate functions in the future. The first is the strategist or architect who works with the CEO and business leaders to align culture, organizational design and performance improvement with business strategy. The second is the delivery of people services, including a reintegrated business partner and shared service model. Others wondered what difference that would this make, and whether it would be more cosmetic than real. Some felt it removed the strong tendency for HR leaders to keep getting pulled back into reactive and transitional activity. By separating them, you removed accountability for HR service delivery. While the research was inconclusive, my instinct is that a structural shift may start a welcome debate about what and who should facilitate a Competitive People Strategy. This is a conversation that the HR community need to have urgently.

'The strategic work around people is currently an underused muscle in HR. We will become an endangered species unless we up our game fast.'

Louise Wallwork, HR Director, BAE Systems Air Sector

'The real values the HR function needs to focus on are the big drivers of leadership, culture and talent. We don't spend enough time on this agenda because the talent we do have in the function is often getting dragged into tactical and operational issues. We need to try something different.'

Kathryn Pritchard, Group Chief People and Strategic Programmes Officer, Odeon

PEOPLE TRANSFORMATION TOOLKIT

1. HR structure

It is important that HR recognizes that, going forward, a one-size approach to structure no longer works. The Ulrich Three Box Model still has much to commend it, but it needs to evolve based on organizations' competitive positioning and business operating model.

Here is a checklist of the things to consider when thinking about how you organize the people function to deliver your Competitive People Strategy:

- Develop a well-articulated Competitive People Strategy. This should describe long-term, organization-wide change with defined business outcomes and measures.

- Review whether a separate people strategist/architect role would provide more value in your organization by losing accountability for HR operations. The greater the need for business transformation (the retail sector, for example), the more attractive this proposition becomes. Make sure the structure of HR fits your business strategy and your business operating model.

- Develop a comprehensive articulation of the skills, capability and mindset needed for each part of your HR function.

2. HR capability

There is a huge opportunity to develop the capability and skills needed for the HR function to up its game, become strategic and add more value:

- Once you have decided on your HR structure and the broad requirements for each team within the structure (see above), develop aspirational role profiles for all HR roles and future proof them by including skill, competence, attitude and mindset.

- Undertake an assessment of the learning gap between current capability the people in role and your desired future state. This may be alarming, but you need to get the team right before you embark on your transformational journey.

- Put in place a people strategy for the HR function itself. Ensure it defines a build, buy or rent approach to transforming the function's capability.

- Develop a robust and comprehensive EVP to attract great HR talent who are higher-quality new entrants that can be developed over time.
- Bring in different talent. Seek to hire strategy consultants, business leaders and data analysts. They will all have to go through an HR learning curve but at least you are starting with the right raw material; the HR skills can be taught but getting the right level of energy and attitude is more important.
- Create a tailored HR development programme with modules on business, change, data, organizational development, leadership and culture. In addition to the hard content, ensure self-development modules are included (eg coaching). On top of the business and transformational development, focus on softer but important learning around personal style, self-esteem, having difficult conversations and giving constructive feedback. The third element of the development programme should include external visits and the creation of an ongoing external mentoring relationship.

3. Business leaders and managers

HR leaders have two separate but related areas of leadership development. The first is that of CEOs, boards and business leaders being educated as to the importance of people's contribution to business success and the types of leadership and cultural interventions that can make a significant impact on performance. This type of intervention needs to be very well designed and tailored to the specific business context. It has to feel relevant and real.

The second is the ongoing need to educate, developing and enhancing the people skill of line managers so they become better coaches who can give strength-based feedback, develop teams and then use data to lead their people more effectively.

Assess line managers against a robust and validated capability profile. Then provide rigorous feedback and development. Reassess them every year for a three-year period. This should include 360 degree feedback and the ongoing quarterly people satisfaction survey. This will provide enough feedback from the team to learn how to improve. The key is the trend; are your HR leaders getting better over time? This relentless approach will demonstrate the level of importance that the organization is now placing on leaders to have great people management skills.

4. Technology and data

It's clear that HR functions have not invested enough in ensuring they are able to get high-quality people analytics and data. Most people functions also need to improve their knowledge of HR technology and how to leverage this for organization benefit. Your organization should undertake a strategic review of HR technology and review market/product availability to support organizational improvement activity. The outcome would be a HR technology roadmap for the business with defined interventions over a three-year period.

Educate HRBPs in the use of people data and test the potential value of predictive people analytics on key performance indicators. Joint development sessions between HRBPs and their business leaders may enable them to learn from each other.

5. The future of HR

The need for the HR profession to spend more time thinking about and exploring the people capability that companies will need over the next decade is self-evident. The Chartered Institute of Personnel and Development and the Society for Human Resource Management, as the two market-leading professional bodies globally, should come together to champion a radical new agenda for the HR profession around the world. This should be based on a comprehensive research programme that demonstrates HR's measurable improvement on business performance. The profession needs to come together to create at least two, but perhaps more, centres of academic excellence, perhaps with one in Europe and another in the USA, to assist with furthering the development of HR capability over the coming decade. Let me know if you can help or if you want to get involved. Contact me at: Kevin@whatsnextconsultancy.uk.com

LACE Partners are running a think tank with the participants of the research and other interested practitioners. If you want to get involved, please contact me at the same email address above and I will help make this happen.

References

Bock, L (2015) *Work Rules: Insights from inside Google that will transform how you live and lead*, John Murray

Brinder, RB and Barends, E (2016) The role of scientific findings in evidence-based HR, *People and Strategy*, 2

Goetz, K (2011) How 3M gave everyone days off and created an innovation dynamo, Fast Company www.fastcompany.com/1663137/how-3m-gave-everyone-days-off-and-created-an-innovation-dynamo

Gratton, L (2004) *The Democratic Enterprise: Liberating your business with freedom, flexibility and commitment*, Pearson Education

Ingham, J (2007) *Strategic Human Capital Management: Creating value through people*, Butterworth Heinemann

Johnson, M (2000) *Winning the People Wars: Talent and the battle for human capital*, Times/Prentice Hall

LACE Partners (2019) *HR on the Offensive: Research report*, June

Reilly, P and Williams, T (2006) *Strategic HR: Building the capability to deliver*, Gower

Rosethorn, H and Mondi, D (2017) *Human Resource/Digital Business*, Prophet in association with HR Grapevine

Schmidt, L (2018) Four job skills hr leaders of the future will need, Fast Company www.fastcompany.com/90206307/four-job-skills-the-hr-leaders-of-the-future-will-need

Timms, P (2017) *HR Transformation: How Human resources can create value and impact business strategy*, Kogan Page

Ulrich, D (1997) *HR Champions: The next agenda for adding value and delivering results*, Harvard Business School

Afterthought – the future

Imagine a world where leaders give their employees enormous freedom to decide what to do and how to do it. Imagine workplaces where employees elect their own leaders and pay is decided by a vote once data on every employee's contribution has been shared with all employees. Let's also think about organizations where the majority of their workers are not employees at all, but a connected group of freelancers living wherever they want. Let's also conceive of businesses giving their people the things they most want – for some money, for many interesting and meaningful work, perhaps the chance to help others or more time with their families. These developments are starting to happen today; we are close to a tipping point where organizations transform themselves as the convergence of AI, machine learning and other technologies coincides with economic changes, including the falling cost of communication. As attitudes towards work and the balance between earning a living and other, as important aspects of people's lives shifts, organizations will have to adapt to retain their talent. People want the organization they work for to do more than make a huge profit; they want their employer to be a force for good, and make a difference to the world we live in. Organizations will change and morph as all businesses, regardless of size, are able to scale globally and secure the economic efficiencies that were traditionally the preserve of large businesses, while at the same time having the human benefits of small businesses, like greater freedom, flexibility, involvement and empowerment. These organizational shifts will change the role of leaders and managers away from command and control towards enabling and cultivating.

On a larger scale, some of the changes brought about by automation will create social and economic challenges, the most obvious being growing inequality; the debate about how the labour market impact of the fourth Industrial Revolution is currently rife. This is not so much about if we have more or fewer jobs, but instead the displacement effect that will cause those who have traditionally worked in the middle of our organizations to lose their jobs. These professional middle-class but routine roles will be eliminated, while higher-paying and skilled roles are created. It's this mismatch of skills and capabilities that will cause disruption. If you are talented and in demand, life will be comfortable, and you will have a choice about who you work for and where and when you work. If you have skills that are not in demand, you may be condemned to 50 years in the jobs market doing two or three jobs without benefits, just to get by. This world, if you take a dystopian view, will lead to greater political change as people who are dissatisfied with their lives look to the far left and right for answers, seek to blame others (the backlash on immigration is just the start) and elect people who promise a return to the nostalgic good times. Governments need to start acting now, by remodelling our education systems, moving away from exam factories to create new institutes to support lifelong learning that can provide training and support so no one gets left behind. There is very little evidence of this happening at present. I believe the HR profession has an important role to play in calling for this urgent change to happen globally.

On the flip side, it's also going to be an exciting time, where leaders and people practitioners who get it right can build not just successful organization, but also great ones to work in. It's clear that business leaders need to understand the power of fully engaging their workforce, providing a great employee experience and developing their people and teams like never before. People create value and wealth, so measuring and focusing on this part of the organization is no longer just part of the job; it is the job. For people leaders, now is the time. This is our opportunity to create businesses that compete through their people. We must be brave and courageous, and take the concepts in this book and start implementing them today. We cannot wait until our businesses are in crisis; we need to start changing our organizations today. In unprecedented periods of change and turbulence, it is always groups of thoughtful, bold and determined people who make the difference; we need to grasp the opportunity. It's now or never.

INDEX

References in *italic* are to figures.